AngelT

AngelThink

The founder's guide to how business angels think
and how to raise money from them

Phil McSweeney

First published 2022

Published under licence by Brown Dog Books and
The Self-Publishing Partnership Ltd, 10b Greenway Farm,
Bath Rd, Wick, nr. Bath BS30 5RL

www.selfpublishingpartnership.co.uk

ISBN printed book: 978-1-83952-537-7
ISBN e-book: 978-1-83952-538-4

Cover design by Andrew Prescott
Internal design by Mac Style
Printed and bound in the UK

This book is printed on FSC certified paper

For every founder who is desperate to bring
something new and special to our world
and needs a little help
in a totally biased system.

For my wife Chris,
my children Rach and Elly,
and my granddaughter Lara Mae.

**Go the extra mile –
it's never crowded there.**

Contents

Foreword

As someone who has lived every minute of being a first-time founder, I'm not going to lie to you. It was tough. Much more so than I'd expected – or hoped – but it was an amazing learning curve and set me up to found Connectd, and also become an investor myself. One of the main lessons I learnt was just how valuable angel investors are for early-stage startups in many ways, beyond the cash investment.

When I was first seeking funding for RealSport, I knew that angel investors would play a part in our hoped-for success, but I didn't realise quite how much. I was amazed by the diversity of our potential angel investors: their broad range of backgrounds and experiences, the amounts they were willing to invest, and their varying levels of desire to be involved beyond the purely monetary. And this in itself was both a blessing and a curse. On the one hand, a vast reservoir of industry experience and expertise that would be willingly offered up to us, a time-poor and relatively threadbare founding team; and on the other, a multitude of people we had to pitch to who were *individuals*, each with their own motivations, goals and personalities. Pitching to angels can be exhausting for this reason alone – each investor will have a different hook which you will need to find and you will speak to a lot of angels on your founder journey!

That said, there is so much you can do to boost your chances of securing investment from angels. At my first startup, RealSport, our first 3 funding rounds were made up purely of angel investor & family office money, before we sold to one of the world's biggest eSports platforms. I'm fully aware that this is the ultimate founder fairy tale and again, playing the honesty card, it's highly atypical. But if I could crystallise what we did right to gain investment, I would boil it down to four major points: have an innovative, exciting and easily differentiated product; be open and transparent about all things at all times; make sure you and your investors are truly aligned – I might even call it having the right chemistry; build the right team that has balance, skill and drive.

Phil dives much deeper into how angels think and how to appeal to them. As a serial angel investor, his knowledge and experience are hugely impressive and have been invaluable to me as the founder of Connectd. To me, Phil typifies the absolute best kind of angel investor; he is knowledgeable in many areas, always willing to offer advice and support, whilst always being respectful of the boundaries that can sometimes get blurred between the founding team and the investor-advisor.

Having been on the receiving end of Phil's generosity and advice, I can honestly say that this book will be a gift to anyone who wants to understand what makes angels tick – and what makes them want to invest.

Roei Samuel
Founder and CEO of Connectd & Angel Investor

Hello, founder

If you're trying to raise money, now or in the future, this book is for you. You are in that niche of people I know I can help. Here's the problem as plainly as I can say it:

- ➡ Your chances are slim.
- ➡ You will succeed if you give yourself an edge over all other founders.
- ➡ Knowing how angels think will do that for you.

I'm an angel. We give money to some founders in return for equity in high-risk startup businesses. Here I've gathered together over 150 'angelthink' insights for you, what we angels will want to hear, see or feel in exchange for giving you priority for investment.

It's not a mechanical 'how to present the perfect pitch' guide. Too many people are doing that already. I go much deeper. Imagine for a moment if you could hear in your own mind the voices of angels. Exactly what angels are thinking. Have you seen the movie *What Women Want* (2000) with Mel Gibson and Helen Hunt? After an accident, he could hear everything women thought. He used those 'obvious' insights to give him the edge to get whatever he wanted. That's the premise here – to let you hear how angels think and use that to your advantage.

You'll probably want to know why an understanding of 'angel thinking' will help you, and what you can do with that knowledge? That's fair. Read on and I'll tell you.

First, let me tell you a little about 'the lay of the land' in securing investment and what I think some of the problems in getting funding are.

At the very beginning, when you have a business idea (and of course it's a fantastic idea!), you soon work out that to develop it, in most cases, will cost you money. You, and possibly a co-founder or two, will come to realise that whatever skills you have between you, there will be gaps. You need a website built, you need a platform developed, you need stock, you need marketing input, you incur legal costs, you need space, etc. You haven't hired anyone yet. The notion that you can bootstrap absolutely everything soon turns into a bit of a myth.

So, founding a business is not just a journey. You'll find yourself on the fastest and steepest learning curve of your life. Successfully raising money will be at the heart of it.

At the beginning, your prime sources of money will be your own savings, your credit card, your friends and family, and then business angels. Angels give **some** founders money – but, to you, angels are an unknown quantity. Notice I said 'some' again. Some founders get funded, most don't. Possibly 25% of founders get angel-funding, no more. About 1% get Venture Capital (VC) funded. The cards are further stacked against female founders, black founders and people who haven't been to university.

Received wisdom is that to raise money you pitch to angels using a pitchdeck, either e-mailed to them or when you pitch face-to-face. They pick through the decks, clarify a couple of things and invest in what they're attracted to. It's akin to online dating or speed-dating. What you must understand is that you are in a contest for attention. The process itself partly contributes to the problem you face – you're not getting attention and you're not getting investment (see **#1 – The Problem** for more detail).

To succeed with angel investment, you need to 'get' angels. You need to break into our thinking, understand our investing habits, know exactly how we tick. You must win our confidence, to second-guess every question or anxiety we might have about you. Here's the nub – you need to make us like **you**, your team and your proposition **more than** we'll like any other proposition – and we see hundreds.

Perception and impression are everything. Just as in any other marketplace, we have to want you. You can and should do so much more than 'the pitch', if you know what and how. I'm going to share with you how to achieve just that.

In your early days, pre-revenue days, you can forget about VC investment. Beware the illusion of choice. After you've spent friends-and-family money, the cornerstone to your success will most likely be angel investment to fund up to your first £1m or so of investment – unless you're very lucky, i.e. beyond lucky enough to get any investment at all. A few VCs may look at lower valuations if a business idea looks particularly promising or has a 'star line-up' (e.g. well-known entrepreneurs with previous exits, or an internationally famous sector expert). VC investment is rare, so that's rarer still. VCs use the money they manage to accelerate existing growth, or 'fuel a fire that's already burning'. They step in when much of the risk has been taken off the field, with the early fallers and also-rans never getting to be large enough to get VC consideration. Angels accept the high risk that most of their investments will go south. We hope a minority will do well enough to cover that risk. Persuading angels to invest in you is a bit of an acid test of whether you're investable – because we know the odds are that you'll fail. Reality check time.

If and when you start to fundraise, there's a lot of 'advice' for founders to be had – some good, some less so. It tends to focus on you, the 'mechanics' of you becoming investable and, in particular, pitch-polishing. It rarely focuses on what you need to understand about angels and what they need to be won over. You'll probably find yourself snatching desperately for ideas from all sorts of sources – founder stories, HMRC guidance, marketing podcasts, TED talks, legal advice, chats with mentors, anywhere you can find anything useful. Unless this is your second time around you probably won't know half of what you need to know at the outset. That lack of knowledge will contribute to the hours and hours of getting up to speed you'll have to put in and how exhausted you'll probably feel most of the time. Reality check time.

You might be surprised by the range of topics I've shared here. Whatever we may look like, angels aren't a homogenous group at all. We are all capable of independent thought! Expect to hear our opinions on sales and marketing, legal, your team, your business model, on scaling, financial management, the competition, global trends, or thoughts about exit. And psychology! You can expect some angels to want to know your thoughts on just about anything!

Lastly, the book title. Originally, I chose a 'tongue-in-cheek' title idea – 'How not to annoy an Angel'. I tested it as a hashtag on LinkedIn with a great response. So I've kept that premise alive throughout – keep on the right side of angels and you'll get the investment you need. Annoy us and you won't. The book certainly isn't flippant, though. It's a 'no-nonsense' attempt to give you sound advice and insights about raising money from angels. It's written in a direct style, a style that you'd expect from angels being honest with you, or in an explanation for why you've lost their interest.

I wish you every success with your venture.

> **'The only way on earth**
> **to influence other people**
> **is to talk about**
> **what they want**
> **and show them**
> **how to get it.'**
> **Dale Carnegie 1936***

* From 'How to win friends and influence people'. A strong book recommendation. I could fill the book with Dale Carnegie quotes!

Before we begin...

What helpful overview can I give you about angels?

- ➡ Angels are real people; humans who live amongst you. We're not sent from a higher power to do good in the world or to rescue unwary and unprepared founders.
- ➡ Angels have the same emotions as you – we celebrate when you do well and get irritated when you make rash or ill-judged decisions. We vote with our feet and, of course, our cheque books.
- ➡ We like exciting proposals – not the dull, repetitious 'me-too' stuff.
- ➡ We like tax relief very much, as offered by the Enterprise Investment Scheme (EIS) and the Seed Enterprise Investment Scheme (SEIS). Make sure you are familiar with these.
- ➡ We might come across as rational – wanting to make decisions on 'robust' financial fundamentals etc. – but we're as susceptible to a good story as anyone else. We are humans – therefore we are 'thrill-seekers'.
- ➡ We have a multitude of different interests, and whilst many may follow the herd / current trend / zeitgeist (what is it today), you may be lucky to find someone that loves your niche.
- ➡ Some of us are multi-millionaires (I'm not!) and are willing to invest tens or even hundreds of thousands in a single venture. They get called 'strategic investors' or 'smart money'. They sometimes get called 'super-angels'.
- ➡ At the other end of the scale, some are fairly average earners or retired people who'll invest perhaps a £100 or £1000 a few times across a portfolio of investments on a crowdfunding platform. They get called 'retail investors' or sometimes 'dumb money'

(unfortunate term – but widely used). Don't discount any of us. Money is money.

- Some angels operate independently, some are part of a group or club, some will work together as a syndicate.
- We may or may not have any specific experience in your sector, or of scaling a company. You may find our advice useful or not. We generally think that you will always find our advice useful! Please tolerate that. Some of us will make good mentors, others less so.
- Several of us have had our own businesses and exited from them. We've 'been there and done that'.
- We invest for different motivations – not just to make money – so you'll find some with impact interests / philanthropic interests / the greater good and so on. You have to find the ones you want.
- People tend to choose friends like themselves. It's no surprise that we're biased (subconsciously) to invest in people we like, and people like us. You could be more important than your idea.
- If the promise goes out of your proposition, we will not bail you out. We are not your fairy godmother.
- There are over 20,000 of us in the UK. (Source: UKBAA)
- We invest around £2bn a year in the UK (more than the amount of venture capital invested in a typical year). (Source: UKBAA)
- We like exits, obviously! I should say we expect exits.

How to get the best out of this book

This short section was insisted on by my editor. I said you'd all be adults.

OK – keeping it brief:

- ➡ Read it.
- ➡ Read it as many times as you like, in any order that you like, anywhere you like.
- ➡ Read it in places where you think angels might be lurking. Have your elevator pitch ready.
- ➡ Do something about those insights that resonate with you. Make notes about things to do or things to change as you think of them.
- ➡ Develop a fundraising plan. Write yourself goals as you get ideas. Change things. Change your plan if you have to.
- ➡ Don't do all the predictable things that all other founders do.
- ➡ Get your co-founder(s) to read it.
- ➡ Read it again in six months' time. What did you miss?
- ➡ When you've finished with it, when you've raised, give it to another founder and tell them how helpful it was. Tell them how you succeeded. Recycle the wisdom.
- ➡ Enjoy it. Give it a positive review so more people buy it.
- ➡ Tell me what helped and what didn't help. I'm on LinkedIn. Let's connect.
- ➡ I've presented the book deliberately in bite-sized chunks, letting you dip in wherever and whenever you want. None of the bites take more than a couple of minutes to read. Some are obvious – some are not. I find that founders can often ignore the obvious anyway. With over 150 bites you will find good value. I'll thank my editor now!

Insights #1 to #150

#1 – The Problem (a)

From a founder's perspective I see lots of problems, or challenges if you will. As I said, most founders don't get funded. Some persist, some 'bootstrap', some succeed, some give up. Let me be right upfront – some business ideas shouldn't be funded. But many that should succeed don't achieve it – because of the way they go about it. I'll mention two problems in particular here, (a) and (b). The content of Angelthink will certainly help you with both.

The first specific problem is partly one of our own making, or at least we perpetuate it. It's to do with what founders do, what you're encouraged to do, what 'rules' you believe you should follow, what you're led to expect will happen, and the gap that exists between all that and what angels actually think.

Founders have been led to believe, or believe it for their own convenience, that the way to introduce themselves to angels is with a pitchdeck – using a pitchdeck almost as a business card. Invariably that means founders don't get close enough to angels, they don't find out how angels think and therefore can't influence that to their own benefit. There's no 'dance' or warm-up in the relationship. It's the pitchdeck 'performance' or 'circus', and 'that's the way things are done around here'. It serves founders so poorly, yet we persist in doing it. A face-to-face pitch lasts 10 minutes max. You might get asked three questions. If you email a pitch then, on average, an angel spends 3 minutes 44 seconds reading it. Everything rides on that one touchpoint. It's like 'Gladiators' or 'Britain's Got Talent' for entrepreneurs. If your pitchdeck performance fails, or you don't even get an audition, then you fail.

Too many founders fail to raise funds. If you can do more to influence how angels think about you, their perception of you, their understanding of your proposition – not just with the pitchdeck (which has to be good) – you massively improve your chances of being funded. No-one ever said you have to stay within the tramlines. An angel, on average, invests in about 1 in 40 of the businesses they see. Let's see if we can **make that one you**.

#1 – The Problem (b)

Secondly, it's widely known that many of the reasons founders don't get funded are due to structural faults in 'the system'. These are difficult for you to influence. The system funds well-educated, white males more than anyone else, and it is gatekept by the same. There are very low levels of success in securing funding by female founders[*], black founders and those who haven't been to university. It might be

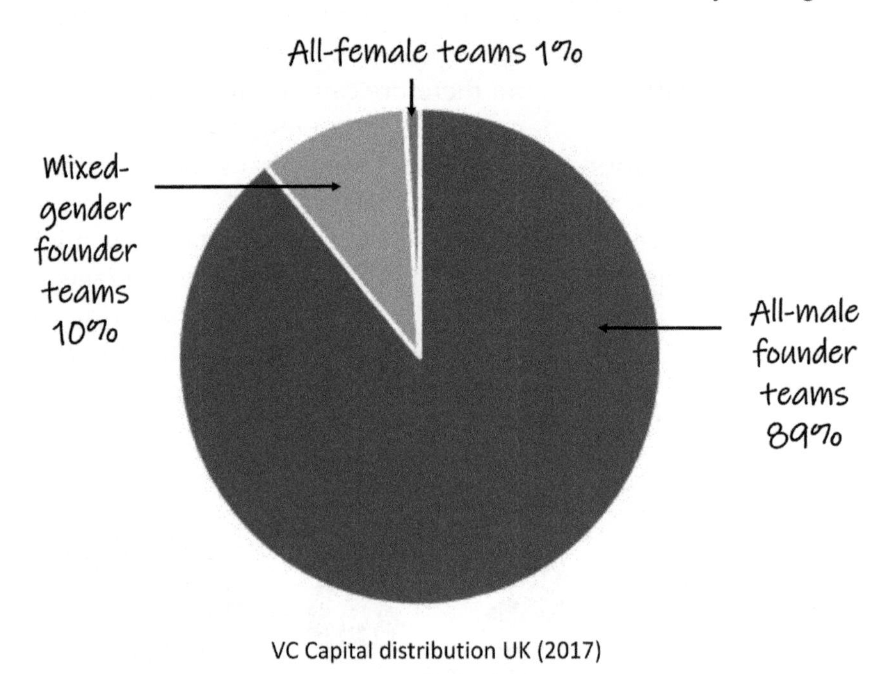

VC Capital distribution UK (2017)

* See also the Rose Review from the NatWest Group.

getting better slowly, but these groups are seriously disadvantaged. Data on this is better for VC funding than angel investment. In 2020 across Europe 90.8% of VC funding went to all-male teams. In the UK just 7% of VC-funded founders did not go to university. Research by the British Business Bank in 2017 found that all-female founders received less than 1% of VC funding.

Only 10 female black founders had received VC funding between 2009 and 2019 in the UK. Google's Black Founder's Fund is beginning to redress the imbalance.

It's a 'Fish can't see the water' kind of problem. It's not really helped by founders pointing it out to investors that they are being overlooked or ignored. What can you do if you are disadvantaged? Find angels that have invested in people like you, in businesses like yours. There are all-female angel groups and black angel groups. Talk to the few VCs that actively state they support diversity. Find founders like you that have succeeded in raising investment and ask them to tell you how. Make the absolute best case you can for your business. Create really exciting businesses. Build sound relationships with the right people – and don't rush.

> **'When dealing with people,**
> **let us remember**
> **we are not dealing**
> **with creatures of logic.**
> **We are dealing with**
> **creatures of emotion,**
> **creatures bristling with**
> **prejudices and motivated by**
> **pride and vanity.'**
>
> **Dale Carnegie 1936**

#2 – Can you excite?

Dear founder,
I want you to excite me. If you want my money then make it exciting for me.
Angel xxx

Yes, I'm being provocative – so let's consider rollercoasters! Kingda Ka (Six Flags Great Adventure Park, USA) holds the records for the highest rollercoaster (456ft) and the longest drop length (418ft). Formula Rossa (Ferrari World Abu Dhabi) is the fastest (149mph). People flock to them – we are all thrillseekers, even angels. I draw the line at the above though! Most of us have 'safe money' – i.e. in premium bonds – and 'play money' to invest with. As a founder you're always asking angels to 'speculate to accumulate'. If we're going to invest in you, then we might talk about safety but, chances are, it won't be our topmost concern. My advice here, then, is give investors a bit of spice. Give us some zest. Tell us why it could be thrillingly exciting to be on your journey with you. Please don't bore me!

I was thinking recently about the Age of Enlightenment (as you do) – the intellectual and philosophical movement that dominated Europe in the 17th and 18th centuries. The history of civilisation seems to be marked by these great leaps forward. Why mention it – because I sense we're entering another one. We've had Klaus Schwab (WEF) name the Fourth Industrial Revolution; we've having the pandemic 'kicker' to technology and new business startups; we're into the 'great resignation'. Everywhere I look I hear talk of AI, Web3, the metaverse, NFTs, etc. The UK startup sector is booming. A study by UHY shows 726,000 new businesses were created in the UK in 2020 (636,000 in 2019). In 2021 UK tech companies made up 38% of the combined valuation of European unicorns – the highest percentage across Europe (i5invest report). There are plenty of 'soonicorns' in the pipeline too (soon-to-be-unicorns). Fintech is leading the charge at the moment.

Founders – with all this frenzied interest and activity, all this choice for angel investment, you're going to have to come up with the very best ideas to successfully raise. There's the challenge before you, then. Can you excite?

Let me tell you about the 'circus'.
You are the performers,
investors pack the crowd.
They sit through the 10-minute acts,
performing poodles,
a bare-chested fire-eater,
clowns throwing buckets
of confetti over each other.
But what do they really want?
They want to see
the high-wire act
– ideally with no safety net –
because that's the headline act.
That's what excites them.
Ask any kid if they want to ride a tricycle
or be a trapeze artist
and you'll have your answer.

(Note: See how I am using 'metaphor' here – the rollercoaster, the circus, the high-wire act – as a way of explaining excitement for angels. Can you find a simple and accurate metaphor or analogy to explain what your business does? One that can cut through a lot of complex description?)

#3 – An investor's hierarchy of needs

Everyone remembers Maslow – even as small children we learnt how to write 'LOVE' and draw a staircase. In 1943 he published possibly the most-cited psychological theory ever – the idea that we're all motivated by five basic categories of needs: physiological, safety, love, esteem and self-actualisation, and that our higher needs begin to emerge as our lower needs get satisfied. It has informed management ideas for motivating staff for generations.

So, I asked myself whether founders might find this motivation theory helpful in understanding and influencing angels? You might take the view that angels would invest only when their physiological and safety needs were met, and that investing would give them some sense of connection, some respect, recognition, self-esteem and so on. I'd buy all that.

But I enjoyed taking a different look at it, as shown in the hierarchy below. Here investors must have the minimum base level needs met first, then they'll look at how relatable the team is, their strengths and enthusiasm. That will make it seem safer. If happy with those, they'll want proof of concept as a minimum and some traction being shown (love and belongingness?). Next, you must show strength in the proposition by likelihood of scaling, breaking even and becoming profitable – the 'esteem' in the proposal. Lastly, self-actualisation equates to 'the best an investment can be', i.e. really strong growth and profitability, giving a strong exit potential and preferably an exit. Actually I'm rather liking this idea, so over to you.

Can you to demonstrate that your proposition delivers against a set of investor needs that strongly motivate? Can you take investors over and above their 'base needs'? Can you, as Dale Carnegie said, give investors what they want?

(Note: I thought I'd try a more complex analogy – Using Maslow's hierarchy to explain an investor's needs. It's easy to do with the right idea.)

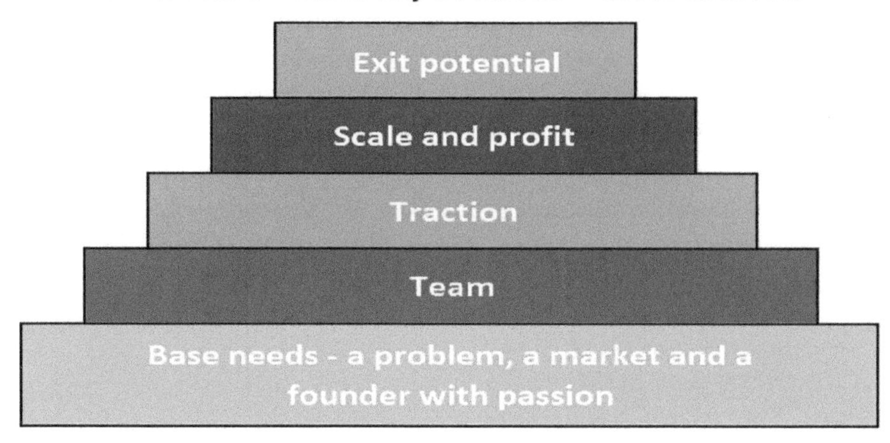

Everyone remembers Maslow – even as small children we learnt how to write 'love' and draw a staircase.

#4 – Where do I begin?

OK – I have a number of bugbears. Let's call this first one 'communication'. When I learnt about communication I always understood it to be a two-way process – there are two senders and two receivers. The sender sends a message, the receiver receives it, the receiver replies (usually conveying they understand), the sender conveys they understand, there's a shared understanding. In effective communication, both parties consent to the exchange taking place and their understanding of each other's position. It works best if both parties fully engage.

Communication to angels, however, seems to have been truncated to something like this:

- founder finds angel on LinkedIn
- founder connects and drops pitch-bombs onto the angel with a deck, and a message saying 'Hello, [complete stranger but angel]. Please look at my fabulous pitch, please invest or please come back to me with any questions.'

Three days later the founder sends another message to you ('Hi! Just bringing this to the top of your inbox!' – how irritating is that!) asking why they haven't heard from you. Do you want to invest? It's all so wrong! The deck may communicate the business idea quite well – that's a start – but other than that it's just plain old cold-calling.

Try warming me up! Look and see if your business is even remotely the kind of thing I have any connection with, or that I've posted about in the past, or if I have contacts who do, or have a role with at the present time. Find something of mutual interest to engage in with me.

Otherwise, prepare for me to ignore you.

#5 – First impressions

Let's talk about you. Initially I might only see you for 10 minutes at a pitching session. It's said that we form our first impressions of people in as short a time as three seconds. You may not even have spoken. Let's assume I can be objective and can suspend judgement for a little longer (I'm clearly a rare specimen). How many decisions do you think I have to make in that time to decide whether I might invest in you?

Put the business idea aside for a moment. What 'evidence' will I be looking for about you? I'll want to know what's driving you, your values, your story, your passion, where has this business idea come from? Tell me that you have a vision for your business, that you're resilient, infinitely flexible, astute, can lead people, and you know and are committed to a potentially arduous journey. Every sense I have will be picking up 'data' about you. I'll make judgements about you from the simplest things – your movements, your smile, your demeanour, eye contact, what you're wearing. I can't help myself. It's heuristics. That'll be you, pigeon-holed. So, can you 'move' me? To be frank, I'll probably be less impressed by your PowerPoint skills than anything else. Think on that.

I'll make judgements about you
from the simplest things –
your movements,
your smile,
your demeanour,
eye contact,
what you're wearing.
That'll be you, pigeon-holed.

#6 – Don't 'disruptive' me, please!

Here's a tip to keep me calm. Don't tell me your business is 'disruptive' when it isn't. Disruptive in business doesn't mean you'll make a big splash. Disruptive isn't the same as innovative. Disruption, or disruptive innovation (full term after Clayton Christensen), starts with a new market entrant identifying a gap in the market, like a population segment that's been overlooked. The new entrant offers an alternative product or service that's more affordable and convenient, reaching customers that had previously been ignored. Lower-performing or less profitable spaces are the low-hanging fruit that give the newco a toehold in the market. By continuous innovation and improvement, the disruptor breaks into the wider market. With a better product and understanding of customer experience, the newco pushes established players out of the market. Market incumbents tend to make the mistake of not acknowledging the threat of the new entrant until it is too late.

Take Wikipedia as an example – initially an underrated idea, it took 11 years of development and refinement to replace the traditional Encyclopaedia Britannica in 2012. Take Aldi as another example – cheaper, unknown but good quality brands, smaller inventory, smaller floor area. Now the major supermarket chains are trying to price match with Aldi. Or Netflix? Yes, look at how they started.

Don't get me wrong; angels love a truly disruptive business, but please use the term in the right way. Otherwise it's just a cheap and meaningless 'hot-button' that most angels will see through.

> **'The four most dangerous words in investing are "This time it's different!"'**
>
> **John Templeton**

#7 – Tell me what you are fighting for – that's your purpose

Most pitchdeck advice says start with the problem. That's a good place to start – but let me offer a refinement. When you come to communicate why you exist, what your purpose is, then David Burkus puts it very succinctly – 'What are you fighting for?' Can you set aside all the various flowery statements you can make and answer that one question. Is there something you see in the world that's made you say 'No longer', that most of the world might find bearable but you and your team refuse to accept as good enough?

Is there something your customers are tired of that you can change for them? What I'm saying here is make the 'problem' your purpose too.

The answer also works for your people. People aren't looking to join a company that's fronted with a fancy mission statement. They want to join a crusade. Can you convey clearly what that is to connect with them? Success – for investment too – starts with you answering 'What are we fighting for?' I want to hear your purpose. I might want to join that fight.

'There's nothing more powerful than a human being who believes that they matter.'

Zach Mercurio

#8 – The real addressable market

It's great to hear that you think you can get to £2m revenue in year 3. It's when you tell me it's realistic because it's only 1% of a £200m market, the market's racing and everyone will be desperate for your product, that I cringe. Why is it always 1%! By all means, work out what you think the Total Addressable Market (TAM) could be, but don't do that lazy association with the numbers, an appeal to simple logic with no fundamental market research. It doesn't wash!

Give me proper customer insights and evidence of need. Build your sales forecasts from the bottom up, not from the top down. Do your best to de-risk those bald market assumptions. I want to hear about real customers with real problems!

'(the) Smart tech investor thinks about:
a) future product roadmap,
b) bottoms-up market size & growth,
c) talent and skill of team.
Essentially you are valuing things
that have not yet happened,
and the likelihood of the CEO
and the team being able
to make them happen.
Finance people find this appalling,
but investors who do this well
can make a lot of money.'

Marc Andreessen

#9 – Our psychological contract

Is there a psychological contract between founder and investor? You may be familiar with the idea in employment terms – that there is an unspoken contract between the employer and the employee. There's an 'exchange theory' going on – the employer gives 'inputs' like time, effort and loyalty, and the employer gives 'rewards' like pay, security and recognition. For it to work properly it must feel fair for both parties. So, founders, consider what the psychological contract is, or should be, between founder and investor. What's the fair offer from both parties?

An angel is giving you money, accepting a great deal of risk. An angel waits a very long time for a return, while probably giving you the benefit of their experience if you want it. What are you giving, over and above equity in your fledgling idea? Do you think that's going to be enough? I want to be kept informed. I want to know what's happening in the business, and what you're planning, on a fairly regular basis. Ultimately, I want an exit. I want you committing to returning my investment. Make it sound fair at the beginning and you've got a better chance of raising.

(Note: Most founders don't think in the way this 'contract' idea suggests. You really should.)

An angel gives you money,
accepts a great deal of risk,
offers you the benefit of their experience,
waits a very long time for a return,
and is often disappointed.
What do you give?

#10 – On growth and profit

Show me you understand the growth / profit dynamic in your business. There's been a backlash recently towards major tech company IPOs with no profit in sight, but if you say 'we'll be profitable next year' you could well be undermining your growth potential. I need to know how you think you'll get to profitability as much as when, and what your view is of more rounds to get there.

You need to understand that investors make their return (via exit) on decent growth to becoming profitable, not profit first. Show me what you think the trajectory to profitability will be. That's what you'll be spending investors' money on.

#11 – Keep it simple

Or, put another way, don't serve me 'word salad'. Of course, I'll want to know about the science, the research, the technology that drives the business, whatever; but please give it to me in plain English. As Albert Einstein said, 'If you can't explain it simply, you don't understand it well enough.' He was talking about cognitive load. I'm an angel, not a professor supervising your doctorate. Don't rain down on me an extract from your dissertation, a blizzard of acronyms, or make me think I'm talking to a jargon-generator.

What I really want to hear about is how the science or technology, the 'magic sauce', is going to make your business viable. What is the value proposition it enables, what's so great about it, what difference could it make to customers or to the world? Don't turn your pitchdeck into a PhD thesis or a Reith lecture. It's not actually for people like you, is it? It's to help me see your idea in the world and convince me that you and your team will make me a return on it.

> **'Never invest in any idea you can't illustrate with a crayon.'**
>
> **Peter Lynch**
> **Fidelity Investments**

#12 – Be prepared

If you get given 10 minutes, rarely more, to pitch in front of investors, then use the time well. Prepare properly, rehearse your pitch, be as fluent as you can be. Make sure you can tell a great growth story underpinned by a robust strategy and sound numbers. Everyone will tell you 'Know your numbers'. Yes, that's true – and make sure they are internally consistent, e.g. that your sales assumptions and prices carry through accurately to your financial projections. Get help to put your pitch together if you're uncertain. Get feedback on it before you pitch for real. Anticipate questions you could be asked and have answers for them prepared.

You just can't show 40 slides in 10 minutes and expect the audience to take it in. Go for a maximum of 12. OK, 15 absolute tops! Make every slide and every word count. In addition to that, make sure you have all the other documents ready that investors will ask you for – such as your articles, a draft shareholder's agreement, more detailed financial projections, full business plan, marketing strategy. It's increasingly fashionable to put them into a 'data room'. If I'm interested when you pitch, I'll expect you to produce these quickly.

#13 – Financial projections

Please don't use the fact that everyone says financial projections are a fiction for not trying to produce a set. I need you to convince me you've put time into working out some fundamentals, like cost of goods, cost of sales and marketing, sales volumes as realistic as you can make them, that you know what it will take in your business to fund growth / scaling. Show me you at least understand the discipline of a financial projection, if not the accuracy. I need to be reassured that when you get to your £2m sales and your £10m sales that you have at least considered the workforce you'll need, what roles you've included, what your payroll and overhead costs could be, what the cost of goods or production will be, and that all that will be sustainable. Cashflow is king in any business. Businesses die because of lack of cashflow. You can expect some angels to be quite forensic about this – e.g. exactly when you'll break even and the amount you need to earn to get to break even, etc. – so be prepared.

Every investor will want to know some basics, like how long the money you raise will last, when you expect you might raise again and how much. (Questions it is impossible to be accurate about, I know, but we'll ask anyway!) Show me you're going to be on top of it.

#14 – Fancy numbers and instinct

Just because you've used IRR, NPV, ROI, discounted cash flow or any other accounting device to make a valuation case, doesn't mean I'm any more likely to believe your numbers. Financial projections in startups are all built on assumptions compounded over time.

Of course, I want to see the numbers, and I'll want you to tell me the assumptions you've made in putting them together. But then I'll still probably use a liberal dose of instinct based on the stories you've told me, the team you've got around you, the markets you claim are there, the competitors, and who else is buying into your ideas.

#15 – If Pythagoras had a pitchdeck...

I feel sorry for all you founders when it comes to pitchdeck advice. There is so much of it about, and I have to say it is pretty inconsistent. I see two broad problems. First, inconsistency – so if guru Jonny and guru Jenny were to write 'Five key things you must have in your pitchdeck', the chances are that three would be the same and two would be different. I know it's partly a style thing – writers are led to believe we haven't the concentration span to absorb 10 things these days, so five it must be. The second thing, though, is that if, say, Elon Musk tells us we need five key things in our deck, our reductionist brains, along with our subconscious authority bias, accepts that's exactly right. That must be the full answer to our pitch. It's Elon Musk saying it! Problem solved.

Pythagoras tells us we can work out the length of the longest side of a right-angled triangle if we have two other bits of data – the lengths of the other two sides. That's been proven. But, sorry, there just aren't 'the five things' you can tell an angel to get him or her to invest, or the exact 10 slides and their exact order for the killer pitch deck. Take an intelligent view on everything we investors might want, choose the most important and be prepared to give it to us coherently.

#16 – Growth and vanity

As a startup it can be difficult to show meaningful growth of your product or service, or product / market fit early on. Be wary of overuse of vanity metrics in a pitch to present the illusion of growth. *Vanity metrics* are measures like registered users, downloads, and raw pageviews. They are easily manipulated, and do not necessarily correlate to the numbers that really matter to your business and to investors: active users, engagement, the cost of getting new customers, and ultimately revenues and profits.

Ask yourself probing questions – like those given below:

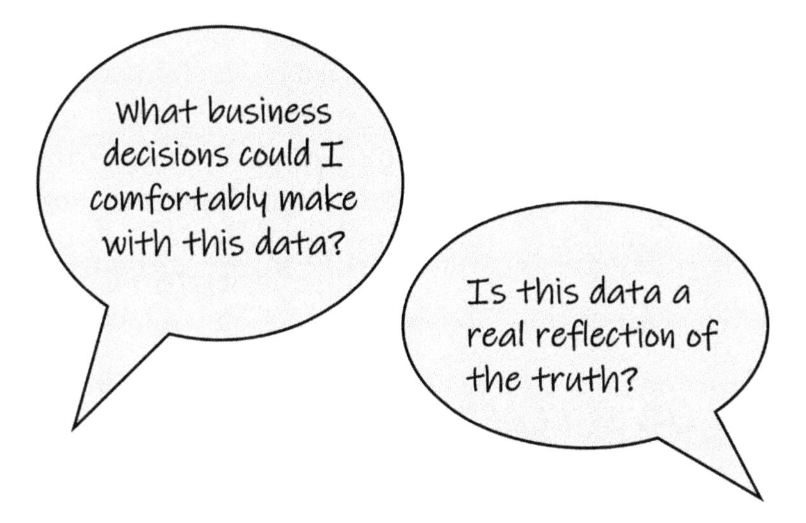

If you don't ask, you can be sure someone will.

'It is very often nothing but our own vanity that deceives us.'

Jane Austen

#17 – On a business plan

Yes, you need a business plan. No, your pitchdeck isn't a business plan. Yes, if I'm interested in you, I'll want to see it and ask you about it. I'll be impressed if you've already written it, and much less so if you haven't. I'd be surprised if you got any different answer from any other serious angel. I don't care how lean a startup you want to be or MVP-oriented you are – if you want other people to invest, you'll need to be able to vocalise a strategy, show key metrics, and give essential projections of sales, spend and cashflow. Don't treat your business plan as a one-off document. Keep it slim, revise it often and use it to manage the business.

Imagine I'm going to drop in on you six months after you've completed this funding round and ask you, 'So, how are you getting on? What's in your business plan at the moment?' Are you prepared?

> **'He who fails to plan is planning to fail.'**
>
> **Winston Churchill**

#18 – On successful long-term relationships

Sometimes an angel is all there is between you and a food bank. Dramatic, yes. True, also yes in my experience. How you as a founder relate to investors is key. You've asked for my money because you say you need it. A relationship is built up over time. You don't propose marriage on the first date. We have to get to trust. We do 'opening salvos' and establish if we're going to get on.

When we get to money, yes, you're the talent but I'm the bank. I'm entitled to ask detailed and challenging questions, have a contrary opinion, get updates on business progress, etc. without you getting defensive or ignoring me. It's up to you to manage my expectations.

You should be aiming to build a successful long-term relationship with investors, because you'll probably (hopefully!) be asking us for more money or to support a vote. Start talking to me like you're already including me in your future and I'll think that way too. Angels aren't just 'transactions' and don't like being taken for granted.

Yes, you're the talent
but I'm the bank.

#19 – Investing your own money

This is another personal bugbear of mine (one of several!) – founders not fully investing their own time and / or money into their new venture. I've occasionally come across a situation where I've been asked to invest and the founder has recently sold a previous business for a significant sum. I don't always know the details of their financial situation, but if I think they're not putting any of their own 'skin in the game' then you'll expect me to ask why should I? Likewise, people that want to be founders part-time because they have so many other commitments – I do find myself asking questions about that.

You must show you're committed. Probably more than 'skin'! You'll hear this called 'all in'. Show you're all-in.

#20 – Mints with your bill? Reciprocity in action

There's a basic tenet of the psychology of relationships called the Principle of Reciprocity.* Simply, it states that we feel an obligation to give something back when something is received, e.g. mints with the restaurant bill to encourage a tip. We don't like to feel that we owe people. This need is strongest when the gift is given without expectation of return. Let's leave aside friendships and social relationships and look at reciprocity in business, specifically investing. You give founders a share of your business, they give you money for it. You give them a share certificate in return, plus a thank you. That is the minimum expected in the transaction. It might feel a bit one-sided, as you are not returning anything to an investor with tangible value at the same time.

So, how can you strengthen that and build on that relationship with angels? Always offer to buy coffee when you meet. Give as much background about the business as you can. A frequent investor newsletter is a great example. If you win a really big contract, send out a bulletin. Christmas greetings, discounts on future share purchases – all ways of demonstrating reciprocity. The reciprocity principle states that the value of the gift is less important than the act of the gift itself. It also states that if you are over the top it will cease to work.

* Reciprocity is the first of Robert Cialdini's 6 Principles of Persuasion. In his book *Influence: The Psychology of Persuasion,* published in 1984, he explores factors that affect the decisions that people make, particularly in relation to sales and purchasing. His work is an influential precursor to Nudge Theory. At the core of his work is the now well accepted idea that decision-making is effortful, so individuals use a lot of rules of thumb, decision-making shortcuts (heuristics) and habits when deciding what to do, how to behave, or what action to take in any situation. You can use these principles to 'lubricate' the right decision. Cialdini is a strongly recommended read.

#21 – Decision-making

You're in a rush and you want me to make a decision. Quickly. I get that. It can be quite a big decision for me, possibly a very big decision. Important but probably not as urgent as it is for you. I may invest as much as buying a new car, for example, one that you can't give me a warranty for or let me take for a test-drive. We all have our own decision-making styles, heuristics and influences. I might be swayed because you are doing something 'visionary' and it's the whole thing you are into that I'm taken with. I want to research that more. Or I might be a wide data-gatherer and want to fill gaps you haven't told me about (that you might also know more about but haven't told me?). As an active angel I'm almost sure to be considering several other options at the same time – so I could have information overload already.

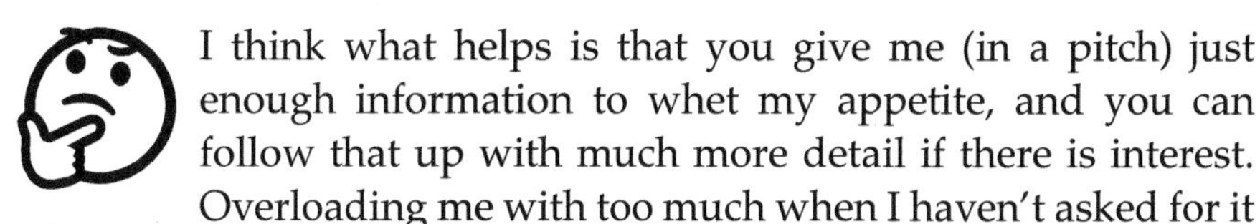

I think what helps is that you give me (in a pitch) just enough information to whet my appetite, and you can follow that up with much more detail if there is interest. Overloading me with too much when I haven't asked for it won't help me. Rushing me while I'm assimilating my thoughts and emotions won't help you or me. Why not ask me what would help me say yes, and then listen.

#22 – B2B and / or B2C?

Many founders appear to think they can be equally a B2B and a B2C business and do this right from the beginning. I'm not saying that's impossible, but I haven't seen a business where I haven't preferred focus, at least at the outset. There can be significant differences in the way you reach different customers, price to each, deliver to each, and certainly there will be differences in sales volume, effort and margin. My view generally is to make a choice to begin with, get that well-established and then consider if there is a good case for diversifying.

#23 – Today I'm the IBM of irritated

Yes – another bugbear to share! I hear a lot of pitches that compare their business to one or other of the digital businesses we are all familiar with – the X of Y. Founders think it's meaningful, or catchy, to describe themselves as the Netflix or Uber or Airbnb of something. As often as not they are not even close to the business model they claim to emulate. Launching the 'Deliveroo of haircuts' with one van that comes to your house or office when the barber has a free time slot is not the comprehensive 'on demand' service of Uber taxis or Uber Eats. Therefore, it's disrupting very little. I recently heard the 'Uber of handbags'! No, I've no idea either!

I suggest you use these descriptions sparingly, and only when you're sure they're accurate, otherwise they can sound pretentious or plain ridiculous (as you would too).

#24 – On business models

Please show me you have given serious thought to choosing a business model. A business model is not simply how you monetise, or your revenue model. It's not just about pricing. A business model is the framework that an organisation uses to systematically unlock long-term value for shareholders while delivering value to customers. Besides monetisation your business model choice implies you understand operations, customer acquisition, retention and supply chain management. I get concerned about the proportion of businesses that simply see the business model as 'subscription model' or 'freemium model' without explaining how all the business pieces fit together. What makes the orchestra produce the best music?

Show me that you've worked this out, and how the business model is reflected in your financial projections. If I tell you I'm concerned that you don't get this, don't expect me to invest.

#25 – On pivoting

Here's a common situation – you've got a small amount of traction, your growth is a bit flat, and you're burning through your first raise. You think you want some more money. I'm not seeing anything different about your offer or your go-to-market plan, or your prospects for that matter – so best not ask me.

Rather than ask for more money, perhaps it's time to pivot? Sometimes only one aspect of the company, product or service needs changing. Before you jump, consider the opportunities for growth and expansion in your new path. If the market is smaller, you can't see a niche, or there's too much competition, then keep looking. Have you accepted that your old plan is going nowhere?

Have you accepted that your old plan is going nowhere?

'A pivot is a change in strategy without a change in vision.'

Eric Ries

#26 – Beware snake oil salesmen

I've had this on my list of irritants for some time, but Arvind Narayanan, an associate professor at Princetown University, has done it for me. He claims much of what is being sold today in tech is in fact a form of hi-tech voodoo, simultaneously useless and dangerous. There are risks for businesses, governments and investors.

I'm not saying that genuine advances are not being made, but I'm wary of hyper-inflated claims and values based on, for example, AI. Some people think AI is just another hype bubble. Some people think the same of the metaverse and Web 3, etc.

Show me what you can genuinely do with your tech please – not what you hope to.

#27 – Oh dear! We've run out of (your) money!

It happens, and that can be annoying! Annoying to me, that is – and desperate for you. There are a variety of reasons – not raising enough, spending it too fast, spending it on things that are unnecessary. More annoying is finding out that you knew it was going to happen and didn't act fast enough to stop it. Did you remember at any time why I invested in you in the first place? You are (were) the custodian of my money. Remember that mindset.

You must have accurate financial projections. I recommend that you have a runway of at least six months AT ALL TIMES. Start raising money if you get anywhere near having only six months' runway. Preferably earlier. If you can't raise at that point then perhaps your investors are telling you something. Sadly, not every business deserves to survive – and investors not following on is a sure sign of that.

#28 – Do you have a persona?

No, not you personally (though I really hope you do). I mean a clearly delineated understanding and description of who your core customer(s) will be. Personas came into use in marketing a generation or so ago to remove personal biases and 'humanise' the relationship with customers. I'm indebted to Louis Grenier (founder of Everyone Hates Marketers) for pointing out the demographic similarities between Prince Charles and Ozzy Osborne:

Both were born in 1948

Two kids each

Grew up in England

Both like dogs

Both Wealthy

Vacation in the Alps

But when it comes to purchasing, they could not be more different. Their demographics have nothing to do with what or why they buy anything.

You need to work out your customer segment(s) by psychographics not demographics. What is driving their behaviour and choices? What goals do they have, what progress do they want to make, and what is stopping them making those choices? Your personas are these people. Real people, and only real people earn you real money. These personas, or avatars if you prefer, are the people with the pain, the people with desires and goals, the ones looking for the best solution that only you have. Show me how you know who they are and what you know about them. Tell me why they might care a lot about your solution. Show me that you've done the market research to identify them. Tell me what your great ideas are of how to get to them. Convince me you know what 'a market' really means and I'll be with you.

#29 – On subscriptions

Subscriptions! Subscriptions! Subscriptions! It's the Kirsty and Phil mantra for tech entrepreneurs. Half of the business pitches I receive state that they are going to earn revenue using a subscription model. That's regardless of whether they are B2B or B2C.

So, consider how many subscriptions to services the average person or business will tolerate? You need to be solving a big problem for people to pay to sign-up and stay with you. If your subscription business is content-driven, how is it all going to get generated? Only the best content? And continuously, I mean. What drop-out rate or churn have you allowed for in your financial projections? What's your cost of customer acquisition? And estimated customer life-time value? Can you increase average order value over time? Can you stack all that up? Subscriptions are great for ongoing revenue if you can make them work, but there's lots to think about if you are going to make a success of this approach.

There are three broad types of subscriptions:

- Goods the customer selects regularly
- A service that the company curates e.g. the best cheeses, wines, ready meals, etc.
- Services e.g. software as a service (SaaS)

#30 – Before you even ask!!!

Yes, I'm an angel and I know why I'm in your crosshairs. But before you even ask anyone for money, have you considered what you need to do first? I'm not going to give you an exhaustive list here, but let's split it into the business stuff and the personal.

Business – have you actually set down how you think your business is going to work? Use a lean canvas approach or the business model canvas – each have their supporters. Get your small team together, go through the nine components of the canvas and fill it in. Team – there's another clue! Is there anyone else on the bus or just you? Have you got them really interested? If not, are they the right people?

Personal stuff – are you ready for this? I don't mean just the money – I mean what it will do to your life for the next who-knows-how-long. Have you talked to other founders who've been going for a while? And any significant other in your life. I'd suggest that strongly before you commit! Running a business is exciting and exhausting in equal measure. Be sure it's for you! I'm investing in you staying the distance.

I'm investing in
you staying the distance.

#31 – On mission and values

'We get it right first time … more often.'

I find too many founders get put under pressure to claim they've developed a world-changing product, or they have a mission to turn some business process completely upside-down, or the founder has had some life-transforming experience that's reset his or her whole value base. Sometimes the resulting output is just banal (as above).

OK, what's most important here is to not make something up. Stay true to yourself, sell yourself on understanding your customer's needs and putting them first, giving great service, hiring great people. Customers will tell their friends about great little companies. Not every top company has declared earth-moving value statements, some don't have them at all. Unilever got taken to task by institutional investors in February 2022 for talking about mayonnaise with a purpose.

#32 – Are you protecting all shareholders?

Investors come forward with the expectation that you'll take all reasonable steps to protect them from a number of possible scenarios that could negatively impact them. These protections should be listed in a legally binding document, a shareholder's agreement, that sets out shareholder's rights and obligations. Any savvy investor will expect to be covered by a shareholder's agreement that the founder should furnish.

The typical clauses would cover the following:

- ➡ Share transfers: a clause which ensures that shares cannot be sold or transferred to an undesirable third party without first either allowing the company to find a purchaser or offering them to other existing shareholders.
- ➡ Drag along and tag along rights: the tag along provision allows minority shareholders to 'tag along' with a larger shareholder or group of shareholders if a buyer comes forward for the larger shareholders. A drag along provision allows majority shareholders to force minority shareholders to join in on a sale of their shares. These clauses give the minority shareholder the right to receive the same price, terms and conditions as any other seller.
- ➡ Share option pool: a clause in which shareholders agree to create an incentive pool of shares for employee share options.
- ➡ Pre-emption and right of first refusal: a clause which guarantees that when a company wants to issue new shares, all shareholders have a right to buy a new amount pro-rata to their existing holding and are given the right to decline first.
- ➡ Non-competition: clauses that aim to prevent shareholders using inside knowledge to support rival activities during and after their time with a company.

- ➡ Share vesting: an arrangement that prevents the allocation of a large block shares (usually to a founder) all in one go but spreads it out over a three or four year period. It's to ensure the founder stays with the company for a minimal period of time.
- ➡ Rights to appoint and remove directors: a clause that may allow a shareholder with a significant holding but under 50% to appoint a director. It is supposed to ensure more minority shareholder representation.
- ➡ Good leaver / bad leaver clauses: a set of clauses which judge whether a shareholder leaves the company on good or bad terms and consequently may either keep the value of their shares or is obliged to sell them on exit to other shareholders at nominal value.
- ➡ Deadlock / fundamental dispute clause: a prior agreement in a shareholder agreement that sets out actions to be taken in the event of deadlock or fundamental dispute between founders. Deadlock clauses tend to boil down to a requirement of one party to sell their shares to the others so that control changes and the remaining shareholders can resolve an issue.

I wouldn't want you kicking yourself when there's more important things you should be doing.

#33 – Fear of missing out – FOMO

I've seen FOMO – fear of missing out – become an increasingly powerful force in our daily lives, made even greater by social media. Humans! We just cannot stop comparing ourselves! You'll be envious of other founders raising more money or scaling quicker than you, or of a friend who's had an exit. I've heard it described as an investor's worst enemy too – we all get jealous because we think someone is doing better with their investments than we are.

I'll probably expect you to play the FOMO card somehow in your fundraise – or its close friend 'scarcity'.* Great card to play, but hopefully you'll try no more than once. Nothing worse than an overplayed hand, like a joke repeatedly told by a comedian because they thought they hadn't had enough laughs first time round. Expect me to be wise to it too. There's only so much FOMO you can actually be afraid of.

'For everything you have missed, you have gained something else.'

Ralph Waldo Emerson

* The second of Cialdini's 6 Principles of Persuasion is scarcity. It states that the less of something there is, the more people tend to want it. This holds true for experiences as well as for material products. It states that to increase interest in your product or service, you may benefit from reducing its availability (or at least creating a sense of scarcity). You'll have seen this principle in action in many different markets. For example, a retail outlet will display a 'Last day at these prices' banner in a shop window, or online sales platforms for hotels and aeroplanes commonly say things like 'only five seats / rooms left at this price'. When raising investment you are effectively saying 'only this amount of equity is available at this price'. Use that approach as a subtle way of creating scarcity, together with announcing the round closes on a given date.

#34 – On the exercise of patience...

In my experience founders are frequently impatient. You have great enthusiasm. You think it's mainly the lack of investment that's holding you back. If you could just raise the money you need, everything else will catch up. Does that sound like you?

Yes, it's true. Money helps you accelerate. The downside is that, if you're not in the best-planned place, money can help you get to a bad place faster. When you're not earning revenue, money is precious. Every penny needs to be prised from you for a very good reason.

There's so much you can do, and do well, before you start asking for money. I'm not talking about all the obvious business-planning fundamentals (though they're a given). I'm talking about whether you've considered how far you can get without giving equity away at all, i.e. bootstrapping, and whether you've started all the sourcing, networking and relationship-building you'll need with possible investors. Angels don't like to see founders being 'loose' with their equity because in time it weakens the founder's position. If you start fundraising and it's slow to get going then trying to build momentum makes you feel good, but it can also help if you try not to fret and fix everything all at once. It usually does no harm to let things feel broken for a while. It's natural, because nothing is ever perfect for long. Chill!

'To lose patience is to lose the battle.'

Mahatma Gandhi

#35 – Investor animosity

I read as widely as I can, and the pages of LinkedIn can convey a certain animosity by founders towards investors at times. We're allowed to have different preferences when it comes to books, films, music, fashions, holiday destinations, partners, anything really – except if I choose not to invest in you. Then, somehow, my judgement has become severely impaired and I can't make any sensible decisions any more. LinkedIn has a big founder community and you might feel better for sounding off there. That's fine, if it's not personalised. I'm not going to leap to the defence of angels either. We're all human, we make good and bad decisions all the time. We're all hard-wired to make very quick decisions on flimsy data, that's for sure.

Ask yourself what better, clearer (and often shorter) case you can make – because I have information overload too. Did I need that 30 slide 'introductory' pitchdeck with more information to follow if I want it? Ask yourself if you could be more ready for investment e.g. more certain about the market, clearer about the business model, having a stronger team. I don't need to be in your noisy fog.

#36 – Founders – the most important post yet!

Remember the story you're telling. A pitchdeck has to have a narrative arc – you've identified a group of people with a significant problem, you have a solution (ideally novel or disruptive in some way), you clearly know who they are (their lifestyle or behaviours, or the businesses you target) and what your solution will change for them. You know that there are a lot of them (large addressable market), you can evidence that (market research), you can supply your solution profitably, you have a genuine passion for doing that, you've got a great team around you, and you'll make us all a good return.

Try to tell me that story imaginatively, in a gripping way. Inject some passion. Make it more compelling than a carpet catalogue. Then we'll all live happily ever after.

> **'What good is it to have a belly**
> **if there's no fire in it?**
> **Wake up, drink your passion,**
> **light a match and get to work.'**
>
> **Simon Sinek**

#37 – Not another pitchdeck 'formula'!!!

Hardly a week goes by without me seeing a new recommendation for a pitchdeck structure or running order. Great claims are made about them, how many millions have been raised by sticking to someone's formula, etc. It's as though this is the most helpful thing advisers can do for a startup – like advise whether the team slide should be at number 7 or number 8, or how much detail to give about the competition. I allow myself an ironic smile when the pitchdeck peddlers say 'show how you're different' using the same deck format as everyone else. Just remember what a pitchdeck is really for – telling me why you need my money to make us more money.

Make your pitchdeck compelling! The more compelling it is the deeper we'll dig. A really big and widespread problem that you've got a proven solution for always seems a good place to start.

#38 – On vision

If you have a vision then I'd like to hear it (see it?). I want to know how what you propose will make things different (ideally better!) in the world. There is absolute value in having a Big Hairy Audacious Goal – BHAG – a place you'll get to in 10–25 years from now, not next month (read Jim Collins on this).*

If your vision is fuzzy then tell me about your purpose. Why are you doing this? That might be clearer. I might be sceptical, of course – as will others – but 'the vision' gives you focus (it should suggest to you your mission) and, as importantly, should inspire others. Sure, vision statements often need refinement – you can't see the whole extent of the mountain range until you've climbed up beyond the foothills. Please make sure your vision is not bland, vague or lifeless – blah, blah!

> **'A vision is not just a picture**
> **of what could be;**
> **it is an appeal to our better selves,**
> **a call to become something more.'**
>
> **Rosabeth Moss Kanter**

#39 – Whose money should I take?

Take it all! No, seriously, this can be a difficult situation for founders to decide on. Received wisdom says you don't want hundreds of small investors on your cap table at the outset because of the potential demands on founders of keeping them all informed. There's an ideal

* Built to Last: Successful Habits of Visionary Companies by Jim Collins and Jerry I.Porras 1994.

place – finding a small number of smart investors who really can influence or persuade their networks to support you. Here the onus is on you to search these people out, validate them and make the offer attractive to them.

The worst kind of investor is the one that thinks he or she knows all about your business opportunities, wants to push you in certain directions, has no real contacts, hasn't invested much and won't stop offering unhelpful advice. Avoid these if you can. Don't feel you can't say no to an investor if you can't see yourself working with them.

#40 – What will kill you?

I'm talking now, not eventually! There's a great little management tool called a pre-mortem. You can apply it to an organisation of any size or stage. In this context it invites a startup to imagine it has failed, then to work backwards to determine what potentially could have led to that failure. Here's how to do it. Look at the situation you expect to be in in two or three years' time, assume you didn't get there and ask yourself why. Get the senior team to do it together. I like every startup team to stress test their assumptions. Most don't. What's the worst that can happen? How prepared are you for that?

Expect angel investors to explore these questions. I will. It might come as 'what's your Plan B' or similar. It's a question angels should ask about their investments too. I suppose it's linked to the 'what doesn't kill you makes you stronger' idea.

#41 – Go big (or go home)

The maths isn't difficult, guys. Five years from now less than 50% of new businesses will still be standing. Of the survivors some will be struggling, some bumbling along, some will have no exit plan at all and only a minority will have made any significant leap forward. You wonder sometimes why angels bother.

That's why angels, and VCs of course, want to hear about 10x value in five years or a similar multiple. That might be why you can't get investment – because you can't demonstrate vision and scale. If you can't stack up your story to show decent growth in your value, then you'll struggle to raise money. Angels will 'reality discount' everything you tell them anyway. As a founder friend of mine says – Go big, or don't go at all. How are you 'going big'?

> **'The greatest danger for all lies in not setting our aim too high and falling short, but in setting our aim too low and achieving the mark.'**
>
> **Michelangelo**

#42 – Oh no! Not another Chief!

Everyone wants to be a Chief. How many times have I met startup businesses where every one of the founders wants to be a 'Chief of …' or 'MD' or 'Director of …'? One overseas enquiry and suddenly you're a 'Global' something.

Yes, I get it. It's a status thing, a vanity thing – but what I want to know is who's going to make things happen? Who's going to get things done, to actually make sales? That doesn't happen just because of what you call yourself. I want to hear how founders will concentrate on delivery first before they worry about what their LinkedIn profile says or how many people they'll be in charge of.

#43 – Valuation (a)

I've got so far into this series without mentioning valuation. Well, that's partly because it's tricky. Many commentators will advise that valuation of a startup is more art than science. There are acknowledged approaches for valuing an established business, like EBITDA multiples for different sectors. For a startup you've probably got no assets and are likely to be generating no revenue at all. It can be a big leap of faith.

The most common approach used here is the 'what's best for me' valuation – where you, the founder, come in high for your reasons and I, the investor, come in low for my reasons – each perfectly valid from our own perspective. So we dance around to find a middle ground, or there's no deal and you have to find someone else. Prepare to talk with a lot of funders. Prepare to say no sometimes. Prepare to be realistic.

#44 – Valuation (b)

Why is it so tricky for startups? To my mind it's about risks and discounts. I was recently talking with a founder who believes his business will be worth £12m in five years' time, mainly if, and there are a load of ifs, sales reach a certain level. Today he hasn't got a customer, he hasn't made one sale, he hasn't proven there is any real interest in the product. His solution saves the customer money, but it requires a complete switch in behaviour of all of a company's workers to a new process.

So we have to agree the risks. You might fail on so many fronts, and we have to agree how you'll discount back from that future valuation to what is reasonable now and where you are today. I say, don't make me point out all the risks and you deny them. That just irritates me. Be fair-minded and we can do a deal.

'Price is what you pay.
Value is what you get.'

Warren Buffet

#45 - So you're going to start personal branding...

The notion of personal branding was coined by Tom Peters in 1997 when he described us as all being the CEO of our own personal brand. You'll have been personal branding continuously – sending messages out into the world all the time – whether you've put much thought into the planning of that or not. So if you're starting a startup, and raising money will depend on a positive profile of you, then it's a good time to think about doing it with more intention and consistency (on every social media you use).

Wikipedia gives a meaty definition: 'Personal branding is the conscious and intentional effort to create and influence public perception of an individual by positioning them as an authority in their industry, elevating their credibility, and differentiating themselves from the competition, to ultimately advance their career, increase their circle of influence, and have a larger impact.'

Take it to be about advancing your business as well as yourself, and that's what you should be doing. I should also say keep your authenticity at the heart of what you do. I think I've come to learn that personal branding is about being more **you** and how to give more of **you**. The authentic you. Brené Brown describes authenticity as 'the collection of choices that we have to make every day.

- ➡ the choice to show up
- ➡ the choice to be real
- ➡ the choice to be honest
- ➡ the choice to let our true selves be seen.'

The branding part means doing it consistently, always delivering on your promise.

You can be sure that angels will welcome you coming across as an authority, a thought leader, in your industry.

#46 – What should you call yourself?

What's your most effective job title? Yes, you're a company founder or co-founder, and that might be an important tag for you. You're in a special minority category, rare but not unique. My thinking at the outset of your company is – drop it.

Call yourself a job title that you think your customers will be looking for. Who do you look for when you approach a company? What title is going to bring customers to you? They're looking for advice or help with a problem – be an adviser. They're looking for someone who can make a decision – add some seniority. If I want to buy something I ask for sales. If I have a complaint I want a complaints manager. I never ask for the founder. If I don't get redress I'll ask for the person in charge (MD / CEO). I'm not sure 'founder' tells me anything. I want someone that solves my problems.

#47 – On too many revenue streams

I come across entrepreneurs with great ideas who often think very creatively about how they can monetise what they've got. They develop a business idea that has six or eight revenue streams – each one requiring their own set of efforts and validations. It's like a competition in the company to find another possible revenue stream. You can have too many revenue streams at the outset.

I like to see focus. Let me repeat that – I really like to see focus. Make your best bet work first. In the worst case I see some revenue streams cannibalising other streams – like you can buy a service from me or buy a checklist showing you how to do it yourself. Isn't that daft? Show me focus, concentrate on making one thing work and don't cannibalise your own business.

#48 – On values and 'wash'

Increasingly, customers are drawn to companies that are making their values explicit – particularly where these are 'social good' values. Making Environmental, Social and Governance (ESG) commitments has become much more prominent. As a founder you might feel good about setting out a list of values, seeing investors as potential customers and customers as potential investors. It's virtuous, certainly.

My suggestion here is to not overestimate the value of making values explicit at the outset; few are better than many and be careful about how they might conflict with each other. Decide whether you want to rank them or treat them as all equal. If you are going to espouse a lot of lofty values I need to be convinced you and your team believe in all of them and it's not just whitewash / greenwash or eyewash.

**'Values are like fingerprints.
Nobody's are the same
but you leave them over
everything you do.'**

Elvis Presley

#49 – So you're crowdfunding...

... or at least you want to. You mean equity crowdfunding, not for rewards or donations. Crowdfunding certainly has its place; a big place given that it raises over $17bn yearly in North America alone. There were over six million crowdfunding campaigns worldwide last year. Many platforms, however, expect you to have raised a fair chunk of the money before they'll list you (often 75% or so). It makes your pitch looks like it has great momentum from the crowd at the outset. That's the 'smoke and mirrors' bit. But yes, try it, if you think your business has 'crowd' appeal.

Actually, there's nothing to stop you trying crowdfunding and the conventional routes at the same time. Don't constrain yourself from being in touch with potential investors. There are dozens of crowdfunding websites. Fundera.com is a useful source. Just be prepared to spend time with individual investors too.

#50 – Your second time around...

You've done it before and ... so what? You've grown a business before and sold it. That's excellent. Angels and VCs like to invest in previous success. For me that puts you one rung up the ladder over someone that's not done that. It might make you wiser, but it doesn't make you gift-wrapped. I'll be asking myself whether you were just lucky, had great mentor(s) or you were in the right place at the right time. Did you actually sell your business, or did someone come looking to buy it?

I'll be looking for all the same rigour, the same discipline, the astuteness you need to show in making a new business case for funding, just like anyone else. If you've done it well before there's possibly a better chance you'll do it even better this time. You'll still have many hurdles to jump. Show me you're capable. My best wishes.

'Love is lovelier
the second time around.
Just as wonderful
with both feet on the ground.'

Jimmy Van Heusen, Sammy Cahn

#51 – Your team

You have to make choices about the key people you want to work with. As the saying goes – you'll only be as good as the people you choose to surround yourself with. I hope you've chosen the most talented people you can find. It's a judgement on your judgement. Think about their potential too – how far can they go? Will they be the right people for when the company scales? Have they got the vision too? Conversely, be brave enough to let go of those who might hold you back. I hope I won't find you've given Billy who you've known from Kindergarten the COO job for no other reason than he's going out with your sister.

The really serious point here for investors is that you and your team have to convey authority.* When faced with angels, do not project desperation! Collectively you should be the most credible and knowledgeable experts in your field. Be as influential and as persuasive as you can be. Do not underestimate the importance that angels place in the team and in a belief in the team's ability to deliver.

You can only be as good as the people you choose to surround yourself with.

* The third of Cialdini's 6 Principles of Persuasion is authority. Authority and credibility are some of the core building blocks of trust. When we trust people, we are more likely to follow them.

#52 – Struggle porn? Believe me, it isn't easy reading!

Some entrepreneurs have an almost masochistic obsession with pushing themselves ever harder, with obsessively reading about how other founders struggle, and with broadcasting just how many hours they work or how few they sleep. The term 'struggle porn' has been coined, and some people seem to find it instructive reading. I have to ask myself if I want to invest in it.

Yes, of course I'm looking for founders with a great deal of grit and resilience, but probably not the ones that are constantly sharing and amplifying their obstacles and hurdles online. Don't get me wrong, I'm as concerned as anyone about mental health among entrepreneurs, and the support they need. Great founders manage to a. create their own support network, and b. concentrate on the right things to share and do in most situations and find workable solutions for themselves.

#53 – Beware the halo effect...

... and other biases. This one's as much for angels as for founders. Cognitive biases are about how our decisions get distorted in any number of ways by our subjective reality. The Halo effect is about how we can become blinded by the good in something or somebody and don't see any of its / their faults. This applies to business ideas, investor memorandums and pitchdecks, as well as anything or anyone else. You only have to think about Elizabeth Holmes and Theranos to see how investors were taken in, to the tune of $700m.

There's a whole analysis possible here about the behavioural psychology at play, like 'confirmation bias' (essentially interpreting what we see as what we want to see) and 'representativeness bias' (seeing a charismatic or persuasive founder as representative of the most successful entrepreneurs we can think of). Make sure you cover every aspect of your pitch as objectively as you can. I'll be trying to give my equal attention to everything across the board, not drawn in by one thing.

> **'And because people are stupid**
> **and use their noses only for blowing,**
> **but believe absolutely anything**
> **they see with their eyes,**
> **they will say it is because this is a girl**
> **with beauty and grace and charm.'**
>
> **Patrick Suskind**

#54 – Tell me about growth

I could say **just** tell me about growth – you get the point. When all's said and done, that's the main thing I'll be interested in. Tell me how growth is going to happen for your business. Tell me how you are going to achieve it. Yes, I know the obvious – each widget costs X and you'll sell it for Y, you'll sell an increasing number month on month, you'll send widgets all over the world and the projections look great, etc. You'll develop new territories, fiddle with the pricing structure, create special offers, employ more people, and all of that. You'll have some headline metrics, etc. That's all well and good, but I'm more interested in how you'll organise yourself for growth, the processes, the nitty-gritty. How will the growers (marketers and salespeople) find the customers, be motivated, be supported to deliver? How many ops people will you need to match your growth projections? What techstack will you use? Who will take overall control of these processes?

All recipes have the 'what' ingredients listed in them, but without the 'how' (how you use the ingredients together to get to the final dish) then they're just a list. Show me some clear management priorities, objectives, key results, metrics, accountability processes, cadences etc. that you believe will make growth happen, that make you an investable company. And show me Plan B too.

#55 – So you want to use influencers...

Customer buying decisions can be influenced as much by the messenger as the message, and some celebrities fulfil the message function very well – whether it be Gary Lineker for Walkers crisps or Ariane Grande for Givenchy. Some startups can get a real lift from celebrity endorsement – George Clooney, for example, sold the Casamigos tequila brand to Diageo for $1bn after only 4 years of brand existence.

If you're going to go down the influencer route, then I'll want to know how you've investigated that match. Are you happy about the person's background and their value set? What commitment does the chosen celebrity have to the brand and brand values, what's their 'ask' for being involved (and does it seem fair), how have you assessed what they'll bring to the business / ROI, and how will you cope living in their shadow if the business becomes more about them not you? What sometimes troubles entrepreneurs is that they never get known for their true input. Will you be okay with that?

#56 – Get me hooked

'Jack Reacher ordered espresso, double, no peel, no cube, foam cup, no china, and before it arrived he saw a man's life change forever.'

Lee Child, *The Hard Way*

Take a lesson from the opening lines of a good crime thriller – get me hooked on your pitch right at the beginning. If you've been following this series so far, you'll know how important I rate a pitch for being able to tell a great story.

Begin with a strong hook – what's gnawing at the pit of your stomach, how you're going to solve a really elusive problem, or how you've found an ingenious way to generate a 10x return. Begin with energy, begin with intrigue. Get visual, use touch and sound, let me hold a prototype. Shake it up. Treat those standard format pitchdeck templates just as a guideline. If you want me to invest, make me notice you.

#57 – On deploying money

Let's be clear on deploying money. Please understand how you will deploy the money you intend to raise and be prepared to explain it. How much you want to raise should be quite an intricate calculation, worked out under a number of key headings over a specific timeframe – IT/software development, sales and marketing, IP/legal, etc. That's to last you until you need more – your runway – either from revenue or a further raise, or a combination of these. It should be quite a precise amount, and I hope you have good plans to manage it. Yes, those plans will change – but what are they now?

Not being clear how much money you want or what to use it for is never a good sign to investors. Please don't go there.

#58 – Remember Darwin?

The survival of the fittest? Who actually makes it as a founder these days? The short answer – not many. Our 'natural' laws suggest it's those best adapted to survive. What I see on Dragons' Den and all across social media are a new set of laws that you'd better be aware of. Some businesses come on to Dragons' Den and you think 'nice idea but can the founder cut it?' You might have your doubts. Can't deny your first impressions, can you? So what happens? The founder(s) usually give away more than intended but what you don't see is him / her / them having a great team wrapped around them. You don't see all the others they're connected to, their web, who the founders can draw on to help drive the business forward.

Their strength is in their team and their wider connections. You see only what the broadcaster wants you to see. Show me the strength of the team, distributed, and how you'll keep adapting. How will you collectively be the fittest? Show me you get these survival rules if you want me to invest.

'Extinction is the rule.
Survival is the exception.'

Carl Sagan

#59 – Don't let the tax tail wag the investment dog

That's the advice of my accountant, and indeed most other accountants, I'm sure. What they generally mean is investors should make the right investments for a balanced portfolio – not be driven by tax benefits as a first consideration. However, where you can be SEIS or EIS eligible you really must take the opportunity, because most angels will be interested in what they can save on tax – income tax, capital gains tax and inheritance tax. Some types of business aren't eligible (check HMRC guidance on gov.uk).

When you start to ask for investment you should have clarified if you are eligible. Look organised. Just a simple step – **and**, of course, it has to look like a good investment regardless! We don't invest for tax reasons alone.

#60 – What's your GTM?

...or go-to-market strategy? No, not a gin and tonic variant. Marketers talk about GTM strategies all the time for any product or service – but it's so relevant when you're starting out. You know what your offering is – your solution to the problem you want me to invest in. So of course you'll have done the work on what the target market is, how big it is, who the target customer is and how you are going to get leads (I do hope so!). Let me repeat that bit – how will you actually get customers? You'll be able to tell me that. You'll have been thinking about your brand and brand positioning, how you want to be seen in the eyes of the customer. You'll be clear on your business model – the best way(s) the business is going to work to turn all your effort into payment. And, of course, you'll be clear on your marketing strategy, channels, digital and so on.

Now, if you have no marketing background, I'll be asking you who you're getting help from. You'll need some input. Clarity is the key. Vagueness won't do. If you haven't road-tested any of this plan then all I can do is treat what you say as a complete guess – maybe a fantasy? Not a good starting point, is it?

'More businesses die from lack of attention than lack of funding.'

Unknown

#61 – People-work and emotional intelligence

You've probably heard of emotional intelligence (EI or EQ), or a little about Daniel Goleman who created it. Much has been written about it, and about whether it's more important to an individual's success than general intelligence (IQ). Many argue yes. In short, EQ is our ability to understand and manage our own emotions, and those of the people around us. It's an essential ability for a leader's success. A good grasp of what it is will help you in dealing with angels. It covers how aware we are of our own emotions and how we regulate them, together with our awareness of the emotions of others and how we work with them. I've no room here to get into detail, but it should be obvious to you that signs of low EQ can lead to angels not wanting to invest. Here are some examples. You know your subject very well, but don't want to listen to the opinions of other people. You say insensitive things and poorly understand other people's emotional state. You blame others too readily, you have outbursts, you want to be the centre of attention. You're insincere, you say the 'right' things to get investment but may not mean them. All warning signs for someone that wants to invest in you.

Are there ways in which you need to improve your 'emotional' functioning, your 'people skills'? Don't make the common mistake of thinking it's all about you and your emotions. How good are you at perceiving and managing your response to the emotions of others? Angels can have EQ shortfalls too. We might need helping over the line.

#62 – Know your market size

Market size is clearly an important consideration when you want to persuade an investor to invest in you. More specifically, the size and potential of the niche in the market that you want to develop. Some suggest you use Total Addressable Market (TAM), Serviceable

Available Market (SAM) and Serviceable Obtainable Market (SOM) as a way of mapping this out for investors. Yes – that could be helpful – except different sources describe these differently. That's unhelpful. For example, sometimes the TAM is described as the whole universe of people with a possible interest in your product or service, sometimes just the country or region. Confusing, isn't it?

What's key here is the SOM – the number of customers you've identified with the need, and that you have (or will have after investment) the resources to go at in that market. Wherever possible, use robust data sources to quantify this market size, such as the Office of National Statistics (ONS), government whitepapers, company or industry reports and online research. I'll ask you to reference those. Then you'll have to make conservative assumptions about the share of the market you can attract in year 1, year 2 and so on. Treat the SOM figure as a point in time – because you'll be hoping to make the SOM bigger over time.

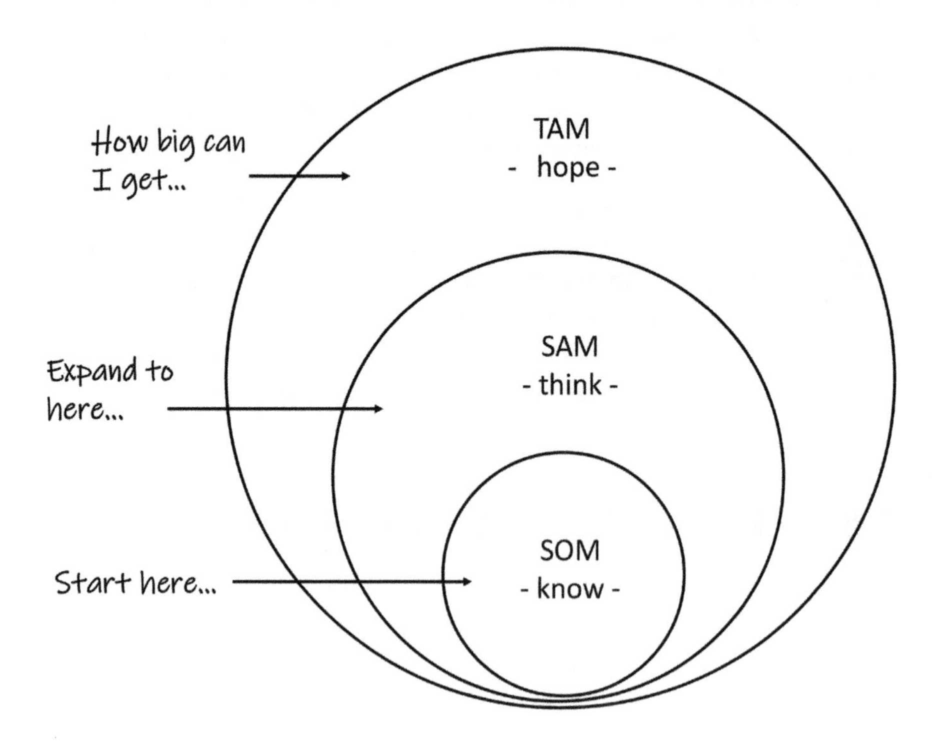

#63 – On customer acquisition costs

Don't let the cost of customer acquisition (CAC) be the killer of your business idea. This is important whether you're an online business or face-to-face. Most people agree on the importance of the product, the team selling it and the size of the market you're in. But consider this – it doesn't matter how good your product / market fit is if you can't find a way to acquire customers at a low enough cost. That's surely a fast way to failure.

I'm going to want you to at least give me some well-reasoned cost estimates of several approaches to acquiring customers. I'm going to want you also to give some well-reasoned estimates of your lifetime customer value (LCV). The lifetime value of a customer is the gross margin you'd expect to make from a customer over the lifetime of the relationship. You need to calculate these two metrics and keep measuring them over time. LCV is recommended to be at least three times more than CAC and preferably five times. Show me a financial model with that in it.

#64 – The faster horse?

Ask the right question(s) about your business idea. Ask for the sake of innovation. You have to do this because it determines how your brain thinks consciously and subconsciously. When you're not concentrating on a problem, a new business idea, or some development of your business then make sure you've seeded your brain with the right questions – because they'll be running round in there. Perhaps you've heard of the faster horse? In the 19th century, when transportation of people was mostly by horseback, and therefore slow, an entrepreneur might have asked 'Could I speed things up by creating a faster horse?' That would have constrained your thought processes – because, although the answer is yes, you've already given me the answer you want.

There's a better question, isn't there? How about 'What's the best way to move people from A to B faster?' That leads you to different solutions – and hopefully one that leads all the others. That's what developing your MVP should concentrate on – the better way.

> **'If I had asked people what they wanted, they would have said faster horses.'**
>
> **Henry Ford**

#65 – On investor relations

Warning! This can really get my goat! If you take other people's money you have to keep them advised about how things are going and what you're doing with their money. The two key things are the regularity and the detail – oh, and honesty. One company I'm invested in sends all investors a monthly report – I like it (because they continue to do well) – but really it's too often. A three- or six-month interval is fine by me. Detail – one company sends me 10 or 12 pages each time – too much. A page or two – just key points – the good news and the bad news, great sales, key personnel changes, where you're going, where you're stuck, any help you want.

Keeping it simple is the answer. Fail to do it or spring surprises on me and I probably won't invest in you again. Sorry – that's how I keep it simple.

#66 – Female founders

On the day after International Women's Day I was thinking about women founders and how they can get an equal chance to start a business. Many more angels are men than women, many are older, and some men are just ingrained with 'unequal' thoughts – how they were socialised from early on. It's possible that the unfairness I've seen in the corporate world in my time is as prevalent in the startup world. If you are a female founder, especially with a female team, you'll want and expect every founder to be given a chance on equal merit – the strength of the idea, the strength of the team, the market demand, and so on – not judged by outdated prejudices and stereotypes.

There are several things you can do – like have a stunning business idea, like look for female angel groups such as Angel Academe, find female mentors, or connect with and approach female founders of existing businesses to share ideas of how they got successfully funded. Search and you'll find answers.

#67 – On growth mindset

I just love the name Dr Dweck! Over 30 years ago Carol Dweck and colleagues got interested in how students responded to failure. They noticed that while some seemed devastated by even small setbacks, others rebounded and progressed well. Dr Dweck coined the terms fixed mindset and growth mindset to describe the different sets of assumptions, notions or the 'world view' children had that influenced their learning.

Okay – let's come back to investors. We want to invest in people with growth mindsets not fixed mindsets. A growth mindset doesn't mean thinking about business growth – it's to do with a willingness to learn, to experiment, to take on challenges and learn from them. You might argue that just putting yourself up as a founder shows the right mindset. Okay, but be sure not to take criticism personally or show that you don't like being challenged. Don't let your ego get in the way. Tell me what you're learning.

(Note: Get the updated edition (2017) of Dr Carol S Dweck's *Mindset: Changing the way you think to fulfil your potential.*)

'You can't win an argument.
If you lose it, you lose it;
and if you win it, you lose it.'

Dale Carnegie

(Note: Don't you just love Dale Carnegie! Okay, well I do for his simple reminder about ego in sales. Say you want to raise money to commercialise travel to the moon. I'm interested in investing. I say I want to go on the first flight to try the cheese. I happen to believe this. You tell me the moon isn't made of cheese. Neil Armstrong disproved that in, when was it, 1969. We've known that for over 50 years now! Does it really matter to you what I believe? I can find out the truth for myself when I go. You think you've won the argument. Pat your ego on the back. And you've just lost my investment. Sorry, I did try to tell you.)

#68 – On 'designer' pitchdecks

I see many pitches. I can generally tell when I receive a pitch that's had significant 'designer' input into it – it's generally very 'visual'. Impact is conveyed through bold colours and dramatic imagery; and it all seems 'vibrant', with lovely logos and choice of fonts etc. Often it's a small work of art – if there was such a thing as a pitch gallery it could hang there. But please don't let that be all it is. I don't need things to be 'prettied up' to assess a good business opportunity. This isn't the Turner Prize competition.

I just need to be able to pull out the key facts I'm interested in – what's the story here, the problem, the value proposition, the route-to-market, the evidenced potential, the financials. Do you follow colour psychology? Most times yellow is probably a better colour than green for a sunrise, or blue conveys trust etc. – but money speaks in only two colours – black and red.

#69 – Timing your raise

In my experience some founders try to raise money too early, when there are too many gaps in the storyline. Be sure you've figured out what the market opportunity really is, who the customers are, and that you can show some proof of concept. We angels will invest when we hear a well-developed idea that is compelling. But a compelling novel and a compelling business idea are not the same thing. I need to be persuaded that you can realise your vision, and that the opportunity is real and sizeable.

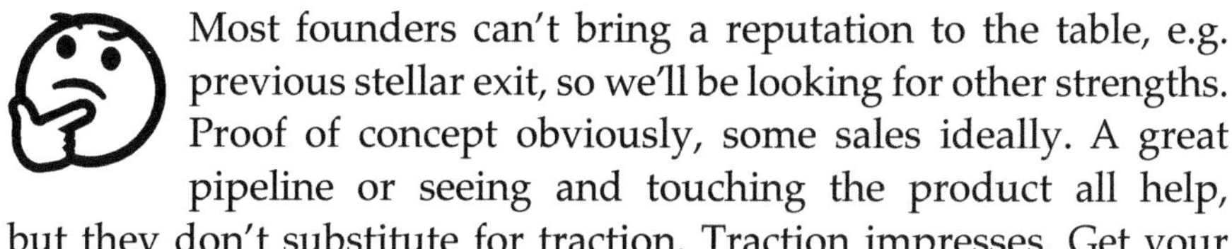

Most founders can't bring a reputation to the table, e.g. previous stellar exit, so we'll be looking for other strengths. Proof of concept obviously, some sales ideally. A great pipeline or seeing and touching the product all help, but they don't substitute for traction. Traction impresses. Get your traction engine running.

#70 – WIIFM (What's in it for me)?

Founders: If you want my investment you have to be able to tell me what's in it for me (WIIFM). Good marketers know how important this perspective is for customers. If I were to buy a Tesla car, I'm looking to solve a problem (or two) for me – like having a really smart car alongside making a sustainable contribution to the planet. I don't have front of mind that I'm helping Elon Musk with getting to Mars or buying Twitter. It's about me. It's the same principle if I'm investing in you. I want you to do well, of course, because it means I'll do well. But, like any other purchase I make, it's what I'm getting out of it that matters. Can you convince me that you really understand what I might want to get out of my investment? I don't just mean now. I mean next year and in five to seven years' time too. I mean that promise of exit you hold out. Keep me front of mind.

Here I will dare to mention the idea of 'angel empathy'. I'm probably the first to use the phrase. Please tell me you got the meaning of this as soon as you read it. Empathy – that ability not just to see the world through my eyes or walk in my shoes but to convince me, to genuinely convince me, that that is what you can actually see, and that it will guide your future actions. Tell me you get what I want!

> **'The buyer is always tuned into one radio station: WIIFM (What's In It For Me). The rest is filtered out as noise.'**
>
> **Steve Woodruff**

#71 – On the number of founders

Having a lot of founders doesn't sit too well with investors. The general consensus is that two founders is better than one (the thought that you can build a multi-million-pound company on your own?), mainly to share workload and avoid burnout, but more than three can be problematic. Data shows that investors favour two founders over one, to the tune of two-founder companies receiving 30% more funding than one-founder companies.

Garry Tan, a former partner at Y Combinator who now runs Initialized Capital, warns that five or six co-founders 'is almost always too many. Four is doable, but often people drop off and you lose big chunks of equity that way.' Plus, 'too many co-founders is usually a sign of a leader who is afraid to say no.' Giving four friends who started the company with you C-level titles and 20% of the company each can be a recipe for disaster. After a couple of rounds of fundraising, none of them will have more than 10% of the company, they become less incentivised to stick with the company and their decisions can be overruled by a Board. They lose their company sooner. You can see why investors might not favour it.

'If you can't feed a team with two pizzas, it's too large.'

Jeff Bezos

#72 – On traction

You should expect me to want to see traction. Traction is evidence of getting towards product / market fit, of validation in the market. Traction is something you can flaunt – if you've got it, show it early. Startups can struggle with this – no sales or small numbers. Honesty is the best policy, but what can you show? Trend growth in revenue, the revenue curve, is best. Showing trend growth in user numbers would be the next best thing. Superimpose one on the other for best effect. On a slide that evidences traction, make sure you use the words that will evidence it, e.g. '30% growth in users month on month for 6 months' or '24% average monthly growth in revenue over last 6 months'. Spell it out for me. Show the trend in acceleration of growth.

In the absence of these metrics, I'll be interested in how you are going to secure users, at what acquisition cost, and what the margins will be. Showing me a pipeline will help, but a pipeline isn't traction. Your confidence level in conversion will help too. If you can show any validation of that, so much the better. In the absence of any of that it's going to come down to you convincing me there's a big enough market that makes it worth it, and how you've validated that. Much tougher, but good luck.

#73 – Hitting the wall?

You're trying to raise money and you've run out of steam? Caffeine obviously won't be enough, you've scoffed all your energy bars and you think you've hit the wall? Okay – I'm not the only angel on the planet. How many have you talked to? How many angel groups have you been in touch with? Where are you looking? LinkedIn isn't the only place. It won't help you dreaming about appearing on Dragons' Den. Stephen Bartlett isn't going to ring you up one evening begging to invest in you. Try the UK Business Angels Association – www.ukbaa.org.uk – as a starting place. They estimate that there are 20,000 angels in the UK, and they privately invest an average of £2bn each year.

I think both of those figures are underestimates. There are hundreds of angel groups in the UK. There are online listings and directories of angels – Crunchbase and AngelList for example. I'm sure there are thousands of angels that UKBAA doesn't know about. I know it takes time and energy. But if you want to raise money you'll have to get on your bike! Pedal up!

#74 – On proof of concept

You want to start a business? You are not alone – 582 million people across the globe run their own business or are in the process of starting one. Many fail, but don't be put off. Many people pick themselves up and start again. One small but annoying snag in the plan – you need someone else's money to get you started. To be successful here you need to give investors the confidence that what you want to provide is something that a viable number of people will pay for. That's called a 'proof of concept' – a definition being 'evidence, typically deriving from an experiment or pilot project, which demonstrates that a design concept, business proposal, etc. is feasible.'

What's crying out to me is to add 'in the real world' after 'feasible'. In the real world you have to have confidence that your business idea or solution will solve your intended customer's pain points better than any other solution they could choose, that they'll adopt it or go through the pain of switching from their current solution. Get some data together to show me this – not just from your friends and family but from real objective users. Don't cheat yourself here. (PS: a pitchdeck isn't the real world!)

**Proof of concept – evidence,
typically deriving from an
experiment or pilot project,
which demonstrates that
a design concept, business proposal, etc.
is feasible.**

#75 – How will you sell it?

Sellers need to earn the trust of buyers to make sales of their product or service. The art of selling anything has moved on – with the importance of being a trusted adviser becoming increasingly popular. So, to invest in you, don't be surprised to be asked not only about your sales strategy but about how you personally will go about selling your new service. That will require not only an in-depth knowledge of your own product / service but also a deep understanding of the problems your target buyer has. It will require an ability to know and share with buyers the wider developments and insights into the market that lead you to genuinely recommend your product.

It's likely you'll have to do that yourself before you can ever afford a salesperson. Just like pitching your business, can you give sound advice that people can trust?

#76 – Will you suffer!

A startup's journey is often described as having six phases – ideation, conception, commitment, validation, scaling, establishing. I might not meet you at the first phase, but I hope you've worked out a realistic expectation of what life is likely to be like as an entrepreneur. You might hope to live a dream and make a lot of money, but how many entrepreneurs have you spoken to about what their life is like, particularly at the early stages?

A good question to ask yourself is 'What will you be willing to suffer for?' Are you prepared for working all hours? Pretty much giving up a social life? Strains on your family? Making less money than you were (possibly a lot less), and working harder for it? Is this still what you want to do? Is it what you leap out of bed for every morning? By the time you're asking for money you should know the answers to these questions. You'll be asked.

#77 – Let's have more cadence please

Cadence is one of my favourite words. I don't hear it often, and not enough in business circles. It means a rhythmic flow of a sequence of sounds or words. It can mean the flow or rhythm of events. It's the beat of your business. Stephen Covey uses it when he talks about a cadence of accountability – the sequencing of meetings needed to ensure something you've planned is really happening.

🤔 So, an angel question, certainly from me, will be around how you've planned to make happen the actions or targets you tell me about, and how you'll monitor that. Are you putting in place a business cycle to monitor who's doing what, what's on track, what isn't? How will your drum beat? You might call it a management team meeting, a Board meeting, whatever – it's what's going to help you get grip with priorities. Simple software helps here, too. I will be asking about your cadence.

#78 – On optimism, and on unicorns

Optimism is an admirable quality, particularly when it comes to business success. If you tell me you're going to be a unicorn, that is most admirable and super-optimistic. A Fundera article in 2020 titled 'Raising Capital for Startups: 8 Statistics That Will Surprise You' provides some interesting insights. First, only about 1 in 200 businesses raise venture capital. They're going to be very selective, usually focusing on specific niches. News headlines skew our perception of this, because the coverage of ultra-successful startups, founders and unicorns is disproportionate. A study by CB Insights showed that only 1% of 1,119 startups that raised seed rounds over 10 years exited with a $1 billion-plus exit valuation.

I share this, not to dampen your enthusiasm but to moderate your expectations. Who says you won't become a unicorn; just keep some more realistic and earlier targets at the front of your mind. I'd love to be investing in a company that got even close to VC interest, let alone unicorn levels of value. Angels are optimists too. Don't ever lose your optimism, but you'll lose angels if you get too far ahead of yourself.

> **'Optimism is a strategy for making a better future. Because unless you believe that the future can be better, you are unlikely to step up and take responsibility for making it so.'**
>
> **Noam Chomsky**

#79 – Smart money, dumb money

It wasn't until I'd made my first half a dozen or so investments that I'd heard of 'smart money' and 'dumb money'. The consensus among investors is that, wherever possible, you should go after smart money. Of course, you're smart reading this, but what is smart money? It's the investors who can bring added value in one or more of the following ways:

- ➡ Contacts to help you grow your business.
- ➡ Specific skillsets you don't have in your team to date (e.g. leadership in high growth environments, sales, financial management, human resource management, programming skills, operations, sales, new media skills, patent filing processes, etc.).
- ➡ Constructive challenge to your ideas and assumptions.
- ➡ Mentorship and coaching when needed.
- ➡ Connections to other investors.
- ➡ Industry credibility based on their background.

Dumb money, an unfortunate and pejorative term, brings money but few or none of the above additional benefits, and usually in smaller amounts.

If you're smart you'll be chasing smart money because of the added benefits they bring. Smart money investors on your cap table are seen as attractive co-investors for VC firms for later investment.

#80 – Just browsing

'I'm just browsing' or tyre kicking. Most of the investor prospects you pitch to won't invest in you – that's just a fact. It might help not to proceed with any expectation that they will. There are a lot of tyre kickers among us, and with so much choice, there's such a lot of tyre kicking we can do. We're 'just browsing' the way you do in a clothes shop.

Don't get disappointed or disillusioned – you can make dozens of pitches before you find someone who just gets your idea and likes you. Here's what I would do, though. Listen to everyone's questions intently, listen to everyone's feedback, ask what interested them and what put them off. It can be the most valuable feedback you can get. Even at this very early stage be open to all feedback, all ideas that could improve your product or service. You're getting it for nothing and before you've committed too much. Sound worth it to you?

#81 – On discovery

You've discovered something – you think it will make a great business! – 'Discovery is seeing what everyone else sees but thinking what no-one else has thought.' Versions of this quote have been attributed to various people since Arthur Schopenhauer in 1851 – with 'discovery' sometimes replaced by 'genius' or 'research'. It could equally be true of entrepreneurship. Steve Jobs once said, 'When you ask creative people how they did something, they feel a little guilty because they didn't really do it, they just saw something.'

So, you tell me what you've seen or what you're thinking about what everyone else has seen – but how you see it differently. New business ideas are often hiding in plain sight. The discovery of the Post-it note comes to mind – a failed experiment to find a glue. Then tell me how what you've seen is going to make a great business. Don't tell me the 'same old, same old'. I hear it too often. Walk me to the edge.

> **'Discovery is**
> **seeing what everyone else sees**
> **but thinking**
> **what no-one else has thought.'**
>
> **Various**

#82 – Let's play 'survivorship bias'...

...and see if I notice. You need to know about survivorship bias because it's probably a card you'll want to play, except I also know about it and I know you'll probably be playing it. Survivorship bias is the tendency we have of focusing on successful people, businesses or strategies, and (subconsciously) ignoring those that failed. We tend to overlook or forget about failures and fail to learn from them. So I expect you'll mention Steve Jobs or Jeff Bezos at some time, or compare your business model to Amazon, or mention a multi-million-pound exit for a similar business. You'll have read, of course, that the most successful people only need three hours sleep a night and run a marathon before breakfast, etc. This may not be a deliberate ploy – it's just survivorship bias playing out.

There's as much to learn from the businesses that fail as there is from the stellar successes. The Titanic didn't sink just because it hit an iceberg. It sunk because leaders ignored all the warnings that they were approaching an iceberg field beforehand and didn't slow down. I don't want to invest in the Titanic mindset.

#83 – I'm not just a label

Angel is just a label. A lot of what I read about angels treats us as a homogenous block of people, with deep pockets, lots of contacts, and looking for a great return. I cannot overstate the importance of getting to know your investors more deeply as individuals.

We often make very personal decisions based on our level of connection with you. Say I want the chance of a good return, and also the tax benefits, but I may also want to 'pay it forward' by helping the next generation of entrepreneurs get started. Say I particularly resonate with your broader purpose – for example, if you're helping to solve a medical problem that resonates with me or my family, or you're solving a social or environmental problem that I also have a big concern about. If you know me better and can personally relate to me, you'll have a better chance of getting my interest and my investment.

#84 – Where do you fit in?

I don't expect every angel to understand the importance of brand positioning, but as a founder you should be thinking about it. I don't mean spending a fortune on the whole brand identity, design and collateral gig but being clear about the place you will want to own in your target customer's mind. Have you found a simple way to communicate your value proposition to your customers? Take Purple Bricks. They used the invented word 'commisery' for 3 years to catapult themselves into the estate agency mainstream by challenging what they saw as the outdated commission model. It's a lovely, memorable hook (to me, anyway) and, though they've stopped using it now, I still remember it every time I see their adverts.

Have you got any ideas on how you are going to get noticed? What your unique look will be? It is really worth looking at competitive distinctiveness and differentiation and starting to choose a route. Take a look at the work of Byron Sharp on this. This is the kind of thinking that will impress an angel.

#85 – Strategy – the moving parts

Your business idea might be fabulous, a great value proposition and with a bit of traction, all good. Now there's a very long journey to get from here to the place five years away where you're telling me 10x exists. You can expect me to ask about strategy and about execution – very much about execution. Using a journey metaphor, the strategy is the plan for getting you to a destination and an allocation of resources to it.

Execution needs a clear roadmap, the practical skills to put a plan into action, breaking the strategy down into operational pieces, and identifying several landmarks (milestones) on the way. For example, you'll have a go-to-market strategy (I hope!), but delivery or execution of it will have dozens of moving parts (I hope!). People will be accountable for moving those parts to complete the whole picture. Be prepared to tell me about this in a bit more detail. I'm investing in you getting there.

> **'Average people have great ideas. Legends have great execution.'**
>
> **Unknown**

#86 – Distort the market!

I'm not an economist but I get this – the more 'monopolistic' your market position is the better you'll do. In a situation of 'perfect competition', where supply perfectly meets demand, the market controls the price and no company has any market power. Profits are minimal. A monopoly, on the other hand, owns its market and can set its own prices. With no competition, it can produce at the quantity and price competition that maximises its profits.

What a successful entrepreneur does is find new markets by creating new demand – like finding a new problem to address or doing it in a different way. A successful entrepreneur finds a way to distort the market to make a profit. Do you have an idea that does this? An idea that means you're not commoditised like everyone else? Please tell me about it. Please let it be a real example. You'll find investors queuing up.

#87 – Crowdfunding – the pros and cons

Crowdfunding – do you know the pros and cons? It can get you a lot of exposure, though it's not guaranteed always to work. You can't filter out anyone's investment that you'd rather not have. I suppose some founders will say anyone's money is fine – they just need the money. About half of crowd fundraising efforts fail after listing (don't raise enough) and it always seems more public if you're on a platform and fail.

If you are considering this, you should take the time to evaluate different platforms. You'll still need a lead investor(s). I find it helps to talk to founders who've used a platform previously. You still have to put in a lot of marketing effort even if you do get listed. Crowdfunding means you'll miss the benefit of some of the wisdom that you'll pick up from the angel route. Keep an eye on the small print too.

#88 – Guts!

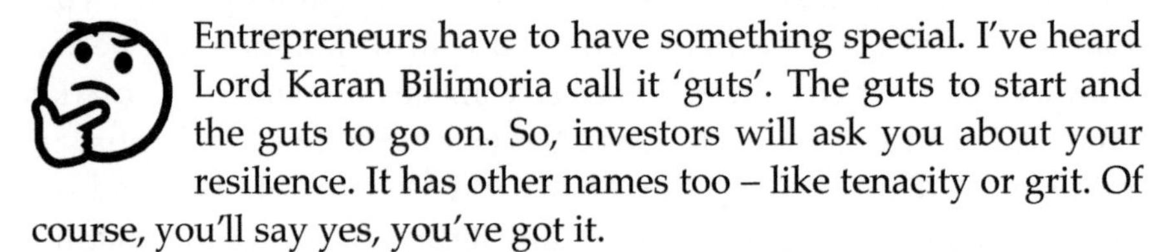

Entrepreneurs have to have something special. I've heard Lord Karan Bilimoria call it 'guts'. The guts to start and the guts to go on. So, investors will ask you about your resilience. It has other names too – like tenacity or grit. Of course, you'll say yes, you've got it.

Ok, so tell me about it. Where does it come from? What makes you resilient? And probably more important than anything else – are you able to give me some examples of how you have been resilient, how you've got back up after setbacks. How do you recharge your batteries? How do you come back with more energy? Be prepared to share what you think growing this business is actually going to mean for you, short- and long-term.

#89 – On herds

Herds. It might help you to know something about investor psychology. There are books on this, so my comments will be short (as usual). The biggest factor that swings an investor's opinion towards or against you is how other investors feel about you. We tend to do what our herd does. Sometimes that creates a stampede and sometimes you get left at the starting gate. When you get your first investor it sends messages to other investors – the first investor has seen something in you, so we need to look again.

It's always good to tell investors the latest investment position, it narrows their focus if they're on the fence. I suggest you don't tell an investor exactly who another investor is until you have to, particularly if it is between VCs. The best thing about securing your first investment is it helps all other investors who are not good at judging investments to make up their minds.

#90 – On credibility

If you want to raise money you have to appear credible. There are so many things that can undermine your credibility and many things you can do to address those. Say you're an estate agent (sorry, I have to pick on someone) and, halfway through your Sunday bath, it comes to you that there's a real need to do something about people's stress in the world, like develop a relaxation app (yes, another one!). You see so many people moving house with stress problems so of course there's a need. Off you go and talk to a developer and start designing some content, wire frames, etc. When you start to tell your story to investors (me and the like), I'd suggest your 'credentials' are going to look a bit flaky, Mr Estate Agent.

No, you can't help how you'll be labelled, but what if you started doing something to change that perception we'll have. You know the thing – like volunteering with a mental health charity, or doing some training in counselling, or finding someone with really relevant experience to work with you? You'd be starting to look more the part. That matters.

#91 – The moat

You're building a moat, you say. Why? Because you've heard Warren Buffett likes moats, you say, and you like Warren Buffett (and so do I). He's one of the greatest investors of my generation, and the fact that he likes moats too is of obvious interest. But you're a startup and he spends multimillions on quoted businesses. A moat is the 'ability of a business to maintain competitive advantages over its competitors in order to protect its long-term profits and market share from competing firms' (according to Investopaedia). Economists call these margins 'monopoly profits'; they are earned because of competitive imperfections in markets. To create a moat you need to formulate strategies that create and exploit economic inefficiencies that set you apart from competitors and earn you profits.

In my experience you should start by targeting new value. Offering people something they have not been offered before creates economic inefficiency. By creating new value you show up the relative inefficiency of your competitors. Your moat is what you can charge because customers can't get what you offer anywhere else.

**To create a moat
you need to formulate strategies
that create and exploit
economic inefficiencies
that set you apart from competitors.**

#92 – On blitzscaling

Mention blitzscaling and you'll make me nervous. Angels aren't the most nervous of people – it's not a 'good fit' with us. You might make me excited but, for sure, blitzscaling will make me nervous. What does it mean? You'll move very fast, you'll grow the company very quickly and massively because you want first-mover advantage. You'll probably mention someone like Amazon or Google just to whet my appetite. I know you'll burn lots of money that you don't have. You may not even have proved product / market fit yet. Blitzscaling means you have to grow your customer base, your revenues and your organisation's ability to execute, all in tandem. I'll be looking for an exceptional person to carry it off. This HBR interview with Reid Hoffman will give you a flavour of the challenge.

So, to be clear, I'm not saying don't say it – just be really clear about how you'll do it – and still expect a lot of scepticism from investors that you can actually pull it off.

#93 – Don't join the beauty parade

Some investors call pitching the beauty parade and, indeed, when so many founders are on the catwalk looking to catch my eye, then it feels a bit like that. Worse still, blindly sending your pitchdeck uninvited to angels you don't even know just doesn't cut it; not for me anyway. You could be a scam artist. Founders believe funders want a pitchdeck right up front – but a pitchdeck is just a bit of formulaic artistry that pretty well anyone can knock out in PowerPoint. The nine-year-old son of a friend of mine is already a genius in PowerPoint – I'm sure he'll be offering a pitchdeck design service soon.

Find another way to attract an angel's attention first, get to know them, get their interest, then get yourself invited to pitch to them.

#94 – I really don't want to hear that!

No – it's not the product or service that matters. I really don't want to hear you've got a great / brilliant / world-beating idea for a product or service. Let me repeat that – I really, really don't. I don't want to hear about your 'killer product' or the 'Build it and they will come' fallacy* you're so taken with. Well, I do, but I don't. Why? Because it just isn't the place to start. When I learnt marketing years ago it was about the 4Ps – product, price, promotion, place – and it was so simple I remembered it for life. It was all about the product first and how you were going to sell it and at what price, etc.

But these days it's wrong-headed. You need to start with the customer and what they want. If you are going to build a successful brand or enterprise, then tell me about customer need first. Tell me that you have a solution to what keeps customers awake at nights. How have you found out and become convinced that there is such a great need there to be satisfied, and what makes you convinced that what you've got is the answer for it? Get that right and I'll be queuing up to invest.

I don't want to hear about your
'killer product'
or the
'Build it and they will come' fallacy
you're so taken with.

* This misquoted line is spoken by Ray Kinsella, played by Kevin Costner, in the film *Field of Dreams*, directed by Phil Alden Robinson (1989).

#95 – On lifestyle businesses

If you think about it for a moment, the last thing a serious entrepreneur dreams of is being labelled as a lifestyle business. When you start your business it definitely isn't what you're looking to build, and I don't want to invest in one either. A 'deliberate' lifestyle business is one that the owner has geared toward developing his or her income and personal requirements rather than maximising the business revenue. A 'lifestyle business' goal puts building a profitable and enjoyable work / life balance for the owner to the fore. Growth and exit are not the main considerations.

If you are looking for funding you must see growth as a priority. Your mission is about reaching more and more customers across more territories. So, show me the business's growth potential and how it's going to scale. Show me how you'll increase sales and revenue and don't let that lifestyle label settle in any investor's mind.

#96 – On Director loans

OK – let's get another of my bugbears out into the open. Imagine this scenario – a founder has spent £50k on developing their business to date. It doesn't really matter on what – the money has gone. Then he or she wants to raise £250k to grow the business and puts a £1.5m pre-money valuation on the business. You think that's fair, you like the business idea and start your due diligence, only to discover that the founder is claiming a £50k Director loan against the business, i.e. at some stage the founder wants to be paid back from the business the £50k they spent on it (possibly from the raise) as well as retaining the lion's share of the equity. What do you think?

For me, no way. It's in the founder's equity stake as far as I'm concerned. Cake and eating it!!!

#97 – Go live, and listen!

Live pitches are always interesting, especially when it comes to the audience asking questions. Sometimes audiences are a bit too 'tame' or not probing enough, but that's another matter. The founder is presenting his or her 'baby' and sometimes someone is going to suggest something could be better. It's natural to get a bit defensive – you've been perfecting this for a while, no doubt. It's natural to try to justify, to want to explain more, to try to talk your way out of a challenge. And who's to say you're not right?

But remember to listen, too, and understand where the challenge is coming from. Someone else might have a good and really helpful point. They might have been exactly where you are before. It's hard to learn anything while talking and just defending your position.

#98 – Winning from second best

We, angels that is, can be a hopelessly optimistic bunch. We want to meet the ideal founder every time – you know the one. He or she knows the market backwards, has started three other wildly successful companies, grown them massively within the expected five years and exited all of them, returning humungous profits to all the investors. We are like giddy adolescents on the first threshold of romance, waiting for the prince or princess to come and complete our dreams. You, unfortunately, will most probably be second best.

So what can you do? You find at least one of the things we want and build on it, play it hard. Make sure you can validate the problem and the value proposition well. Find someone who has exited to join your team. Find examples of other similar companies who have exited at good prices. Get a prince or princess! It's the halo effect – show us one really good thing about you and some of us might believe you can do all the rest.

#99 – Founder's Syndrome

Have you got Founder's Syndrome? I expect founders to be dynamic and decisive, to listen and learn from their team, and to have a clear vision of what their company could become. I hope you have the same expectations of yourself as I do. Sometimes, though, founders have unhelpful traits. They can hold a lot of power but don't use it well. They're often sceptical about 'bureaucracy' or 'planning' or 'systems', and manage in a reactive way, often to crises, and don't listen to anyone else's views. It's hard to learn whilst talking all the time. They might favour staff who work to their bidding, not for the benefit of the organisation. They motivate by fear or guilt, sometimes without realising it. They can create more demands, more dependence on themselves, and can't let go of things. They feel dysfunctional to work with; team members become frustrated and demotivated. They might want to take personal credit for all the good that happens in their company and blame others when things don't go well.

It's not incurable, just another layer of issues getting in the way of me making an investment. If that rings a bell for you then what are you going to do about it? I like founders who are willing to listen and learn as well as talk.

I expect founders to be
dynamic and decisive,
to listen and learn from their team,
and to have a clear vision of
what their company could become.
I hope you have the same
expectations of yourself as I do.

#100 – What you know and what you don’t

When you’ve got a new product or service idea, you’ll be tempted to think that investors want you to know everything about the market, the competition, the global situation, the best business models, the best pricing model, the kitchen sink; to have an answer for every one of their questions.

I want you to know what you should know well but also to tell me what you don’t know – not give me a load of bluff or worse. It’s absolutely the worst thing for founders to pretend to know what they don’t, or to be dismissive or arrogant about it. Don’t be afraid to ask as well as tell. I’m just looking for honesty.

#101 – Be receptive

I worked with two founders of different businesses recently who showed me their pitchdecks. They asked for my advice. I suggested what I thought were some improvements. Each responded with something to the effect that ‘You want me to change it again. I’ve re-written this a dozen times (moan, moan)!’

Well, guys, welcome to the world of being a startup. If you can’t get the message right, then go with the consequences. The founders who raise quickly are a small minority. The majority of founders never raise the money they want. Why? Sometimes they just can’t communicate what a great opportunity their business idea is. And, speaking the truth, sometimes it just isn’t a great idea. Hearing that early is the most helpful thing you can hear.

#102 – The competition

You won't go far before a potential investor asks you about your competitors or the 'competitor landscape'. We love jargon! It's not a question you can ignore – but see my last sentence below. They want to know whether you've assessed the current market and analysed who the competitors will be for the revenue you are chasing. Wikipedia describes competitor analysis as 'an assessment of the strengths and weaknesses of current and potential competitors. This analysis provides both an offensive and defensive strategic context to identify opportunities and threats.' In short – know who they are, know how you can attack or undermine their position (e.g. by being so much better), know how you can defend against them. Potential competitors are an interesting area – you can't always know who will come into the market, particularly if you start making waves. You can't get away with just saying you are better – you have to commit to keep developing your offer.

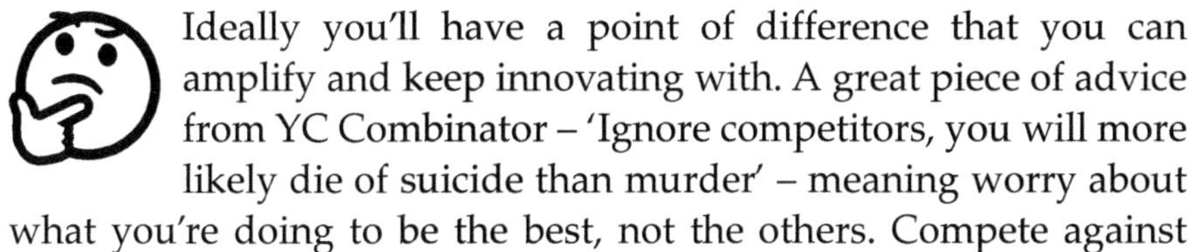

Ideally you'll have a point of difference that you can amplify and keep innovating with. A great piece of advice from YC Combinator – 'Ignore competitors, you will more likely die of suicide than murder' – meaning worry about what you're doing to be the best, not the others. Compete against yourself. I'd invest in that.

**'Ignore competitors,
you will more likely die of
suicide than murder.'**

YC Combinator

#103 – The three types of competitor

Know the three types of competition* you face. Yes – there are three broad types. It's natural to think of the first type – those that offer the same products as you, making their money from the same thing you do. Your sales team go head-to-head with them. They're your direct competitors. But we have indirect competitors – they offer the same product or service but with a different business model. They earn revenue in a different way, e.g. you sell travel insurance but some bank accounts include it in a bundle of benefits or perks that come with a monthly banking charge. Different sales channel, same end-user benefit. Lastly, what about replacement competitors – the alternatives to buying your product? The field of entertainment is packed with examples. Your customers could choose to pay to watch a film, go to a show, play a computer game, read a book, etc. You have least control over this type.

When you think of marketing your business, I find this approach to analysing the competition is really useful. As a startup it might help you decide on the best revenue-generating approach(es) or model and on the best concentration of your sales and marketing effort. Tell me how you'll tackle each of these three types.

#104 – You want the right angels?

Okay – prepare for another of my bugbears. I learn a lot from marketing people. Some of it is useful – like what shotgun marketing and niche marketing are – and some of it I can apply to raising investment.

A shotgun marketing approach sounds like this – 'If we really had a good target we'd aim right at it, but since we don't, we're going to blitz the field with pellets in the hope we'll hit something. Perhaps we'll

* Inspiration from Daniel Burstein and Paul Clowe – a thoughtful article way back in 2012!

come up with a better plan later.' A friend of mine in the insurance industry describes this as broadly what happens there. They know that perhaps 1%–2% of leads will convert, so that they spend as little as possible on the early prospect because the value is in the converted.

Niche marketing – you might call it sniper marketing – is more like 'We'll take a bit of time to learn and understand who the target really is and hit them with a precision shot.' You can try the shotgun approach to finding investors, it's cheap with a very high miss ratio, or you can spend a little more time finding exactly the right people.

I find the shotgun approach to finding angels an anathema. It's the 'blindly sending out pitchdecks to people you've never had any contact with' approach. My advice is that you 'unlearn' it and stop wasting people's time. Crowdfunding is a bit like shotgun marketing, though it can work. But do you know who you really want on your cap table? Dig, dig and dig some more. Ask investors who else they know. Sometimes it will pay you to stalk them.

Shotgun marketing – 'If we really had a good target we'd aim right at it, but since we don't, we're going to blitz the field with pellets in the hope we'll hit something. Perhaps we'll come up with a better plan later.'

Niche marketing – 'We'll take a bit of time to learn and understand who the target really is. Then we'll hit them with a precision shot.'

#105 – On value

Value is another concept I learn a lot about from marketing colleagues. Marketers say value, or perceived value, is more important to customers than price. Good value, or perceived superior value, gives you better pricing power. Startups can have a real struggle with pricing because they may have few points of reference to set prices. But marketing has to be done profitably nevertheless.

So show me how you think your cost of customer acquisition will come down over time. Show me how you'll get an improving ROI. But, from an investor's perspective, 'value' also means how you are going to build value in the company. How are you going to build enterprise value? You really have to get to decent margins to do this, and it's really difficult if you can't price profitably.

#106 – One year on...

Be prepared for the 'one year on' question. It goes like this – 'Assume we give you all the money you want. Where will you be in a year's time?' You can't be certain what an angel is getting at but be prepared to cover off all the bases. Obviously, you'll be expected to know what you'll spend it on. So where will you be with sales and marketing? Financially? Will more fundraising be needed? Where will you be with development of any prototype or software? What do you anticipate on the workforce / recruitment situation front?

Common areas of interest from angels are revenue projections, follow-on funding likelihood, where you might expand to, and how you will have specialised and narrowed down your role, particularly if you have co-founders. You can't carry on doing everything forever. Give that some thought and have some answers.

#107 – Where's your jugular?

Insightful investors will go for the jugular. These are examples of 'jugular questions'. Where are the flaws in your proposition or presentation? Let's start with the problem you think you can solve. How do you know it's the right problem? What exactly is your core business, after you've stripped away all the superfluous stuff? Is that going to generate enough revenue, and is it going to do it profitably? Can you grow the company? Will it be scalable? Do you know the difference and how to deliver scale?

Growth is simply growth in revenue. Scaling is growth without incurring significant costs. A scalable business deploys technology to handle more customers and grow revenue exponentially, while only increasing costs incrementally, if at all. I've used this example before:

I travel from my home to a hotel on the south coast for a weekend break. I have to cross a toll crossing (Dartford Crossing) which is unmanned but it uses automatic number plate recognition to work out if you haven't paid the crossing fee online. The business can scale. That means if it can increase traffic, it can increase revenue without a substantial increase in resources. There are no more people in booths collecting or counting cash. The hotel, by contrast, is quite resource-intensive – cooks, cleaners, waiting staff, laundry, maintenance. Some processes are automated, e.g. online booking and stock control, but much more growth would require matching that with revenue spend (e.g. on adding more rooms, more staff or buying another hotel).

Sometimes the phrases 'linear growth' and 'exponential growth' are used to differentiate between growth and scale. It's important to use the right term at pitch time. Can you do that? Are you delivering your product / service as cheaply as you can and charging as much as you could? Here we're talking about getting the balance right between chasing growth and sustainability. Some investors take no prisoners! Answer what you can and tell them you're very willing to listen to their ideas.

A scalable business deploys technology to handle more customers and grow revenue exponentially, while only increasing costs incrementally, if at all. Can you do that?

#108 – Nobody wants a down round

A down round is when the pre-money valuation of a subsequent round is lower than the post-money valuation of the previous round. Normally when you raise money the founders and the original investors get diluted (they own less of the company) but are compensated for the dilution by the increase in share price. In a down round the shares are worth less and the effect of dilution is even larger. You may think it's no-one's fault – earnings targets are not reached, or new competitors are taking market share, or wider market factors come into play – but a down round is painful because a lot of existing investors lose confidence in you. It sends the wrong signals – to investors, to observers and to employees. It puts at risk future partnerships and contracts and makes raising future funds harder. It could demotivate you and your co-founders.

Your options are limited if you act late – get really lean or look at bridge financing. Or fold. Whatever you do, investors will say you should have seen it coming, you should have taken action earlier. It's a very good reason to keep investors informed on a regular basis. Operate on a 'no surprises' basis.

#109 – Who are your collaborators?

I'm always interested in who founders are collaborating with. I'm not expecting any formal partnership arrangements, signed joint venture agreements etc. at an early stage – just a recognition that there's a lot to be gained from working with others and approaches being made. There's a proverb, often attributed to being of African origin, that reads 'If you want to go fast, go alone. If you want to go far, go together'. It speaks to a culture of 'community' rather than a more Western culture of individuality. It speaks to trust too.

It's always much more interesting to hear you're actually collaborating rather than just being told a list of who you could talk to. Who are you close to with your ideas? How do you think you could help each other?

'If you want to go fast, go alone.
If you want to go far, go together.'

African proverb

#110 – On first offers and saying 'No!'

The first offer you get won't always be the best. Please think seriously about the first offer that's made to you. Don't be in an all-fired rush because, if you have a really good business proposition, the right offers will come along. First offers can have a number of problems, though not always. Angels can come back sounding like this:

- They want to beat you down on price.
- They've missed something fundamental in your pitch that adds to the company's value.
- They haven't done their due diligence.
- They come back and change their mind or are hesitant because they are looking at too many opportunities.

- They want preference shares.
- They have unrealistic expectations that you'll exit in two years.

All reasons to hang back for a bit, or even say no thanks.

I welcome the price coming down, like any other investor, but I'd like to see that validated by others too. If your first offer is really 'smart money' and they are going to help you build your business through connections, then go for it, but don't let your ego make the decision just because you've had a first offer. That may not be the best you'll get.

#111 – Influencing live!

It's very possible that some of your behaviours in front of a crowd of angels will influence their behaviour towards you. For example, every time I go to a pitch I am told what a problem is as the precursor to a business idea. As an angel I've never once been asked to consider what the scale of a particular problem is. Say you had an idea to radically improve adult literacy. You'd inform me that 16.4% of adults in England, or 7.1 million people, can be described as having 'very poor literacy skills'. Why not ask me first how big I think the problem is? Make me think about the problem. Get me engaged. Tell me what very poor literacy skills means – that people can understand a short and easy text on a familiar topic, but reading information from unfamiliar sources, or on unfamiliar topics, causes them problems (this is also known as being functionally illiterate) – then ask me a question like 'How many adults in England do you think have very poor literacy? Give me a percentage of adults or say '1 in X'.

The more you ask people to become actively engaged in a problem the more they might consider helping (i.e. investing, advising). Ask them to do you a small favour – like connect with you. Ask them to do it there and then – by using the LinkedIn Find Nearby function. If they show one small commitment they are more disposed to making a larger commitment, like receiving more detailed information, your white paper or an update, or a revised pitchdeck. This as another of Cialdini's Principles of Persuasion – Commitment and Consistency.*

#112 – On mindless approaches

FOUNDERS – if you're looking for angel investment this is just the kind of mindless approach I suggest you avoid:

> 'Hi Phil. Just bringing this to the top of your inbox to see if you would like to learn more about Blergh's current investment opportunity. You might have missed my first message. Happy to share more information with you. You are welcome to book a meeting with our CEO, Clueless Charles, here – (Calendly link).'

I get this kind of approach all the time. This is the company's first contact with me. I haven't missed anything. I have enough at the top of my inbox, thank you. I don't need anyone else to organise it. I've never heard of the company, the sender or the CEO. The company name gives me no clue as to what it does. I'd have to spend time looking that up. I'm time-poor. There's nothing here that tells me anything to pique my interest whatsoever. Investment opportunities are more common than rain in Cardiff. I'm as likely to book a slot with Charles as donate him an organ. *Delete*.

If you're looking for angel investors, please don't try this!

* The fourth of Cialdini's 6 Principles of Persuasion is commitment and consistency. People like to be consistent with their identity or sense of self-image. If I can convince you to act in a minor way in relation to something, then you'll think of yourself as that type of person and be more likely to act in that way again in the future.

#113 – On audacity and BHAGs

I have to say I like audacity. Jim Collins started me off with BHAGS – Big Hairy Audacious Goals.* I do like a business idea and a team that thinks big and bold. BHAGs need to seem unattainable in the near term. Collins talks of a 10–25-year timescale. They're mountains to climb, they're 'put a man on the moon'. They're like transforming a market, or being the market leader in a sector. Nike began with a simple mission – 'Crush Adidas'. They managed that after 20 years. Then they were unable to create a new compelling vision and were overtaken by Reebok. This changed situation made the company return to its original vision statement of the sixties, but slightly updated – 'Crush Reebok'. That clear goal made them the biggest again. With all competitors beaten, Nike's vision now focuses more towards their customers – 'To bring inspiration and motivation to every athlete in the world'. And Nike sees everyone with a body as an athlete.

Peter Thiel – my mentor but he doesn't know it yet – talks about building something that is 10x better than the competition; like Amazon started online with 10 times as many books as any conventional bookshop. Tell me how you're 'thinking big' with your idea – but tell me this too – how are you thinking big in a small market? Far better to start by trying to dominate and lead by innovation in a specific niche than being an also-ran in a massively competitive field. And don't take that 10x number literally – just show me 'the pack that needs leading' and your ideas about how you might get there. That might get me interested.

* *Built to Last: Successful Habits of Visionary Companies,* the 1994 book written with Jerry Porras.

‘Set goals that are so big, so hairy,
they make you gulp.
When you’re about to fall asleep,
your BHAG (Big Hairy Audacious Goal)
is there by your bed
all hairy with glowing eyes.

When you wake up it’s there:
“Good morning, I am your BHAG.
I own your life.”’

Jim Collins

#114 – Valuation (c)

Two developers go into a bar. Sounds like the start of a joke, doesn't it? They scratch out a business idea on the back of a beermat. Within months they dream they'll have several thousand users. Of course they will (HaHa! I laugh up my sleeve), but what's it worth? It should be blindingly obvious that there's no formula that will give them an answer. They have to justify any sort of valuation at all. It's often suggested to founders that they let investors set the price. We'll have a view on what's too much (less likely to tell you anything is too much!).

I think what's key for you is getting as much investor interest as you can before you firm up the price. More interest means you can push the price a bit. Have a ballpark range in mind – take some ideas from comparable companies and their valuations, e.g. what you've seen on crowdfunding platforms over the last 6–12 months. Be prepared for some negotiation to get the investors you really want.

#115 – Your meeting goal

When you first get to meet an investor face-to-face on a one-to-one basis, remember this – your goal is not to close at that meeting – it's to get to the next meeting. I've never found out all I want from one meeting with a founder; I need some 'mulling over' time. You'll get to judge who are the most serious, but book lots of meetings. I'll expect you to tell me that you'll want to close quickly, and you should, because raising investment is a distraction, but that won't make me make up my mind any quicker.

Investors might reasonably expect that you've made some effort to find out a little about their interests beforehand – do some research on what they've invested in and how those are doing if you can. Try to be as brief and as essential as you were with the first pitch and give plenty of time to listen to them and their questions. You're focusing on making a connection with someone who you're going to have a relationship with for a long time. Lastly, make sure you don't leave without absolute clarity on next steps

#116 – On momentum

Once you begin a fundraise it's important to keep up some momentum. Nail down angels you want to talk to and groups you want to go to. Once one investor has committed, a seed investment can often be closed quite rapidly. As previously noted, it is an advantage to use standard documents with consistent terms. Encourage due diligence to start as soon as possible. Negotiation can then proceed on any variables you are willing to concede ground on, usually only the valuation.

Deals have momentum and there is no better recipe towards building momentum behind your deal than by telling a great story, having a plan and delivering on it. You may have to meet with dozens of investors before you get to close the round. But to get started you just need to convince one of them. Once the first money is in, each subsequent contribution should get faster and easier. Once an investor says that they are in, you are well on the way.

#117 – On negotiations

When you enter into a negotiation with a VC or an angel, remember that they are usually more experienced at it than you are, so it is almost always better not to try to negotiate in real-time. Take requests away with you, and seek help from co-founders, advisers, or legal counsel if needs be. But also remember that, although certain requested terms can seem one-sided, the majority of things credible VCs and angels will ask for tend to be reasonable. Do not hesitate to ask them to explain precisely what they are asking for and why.

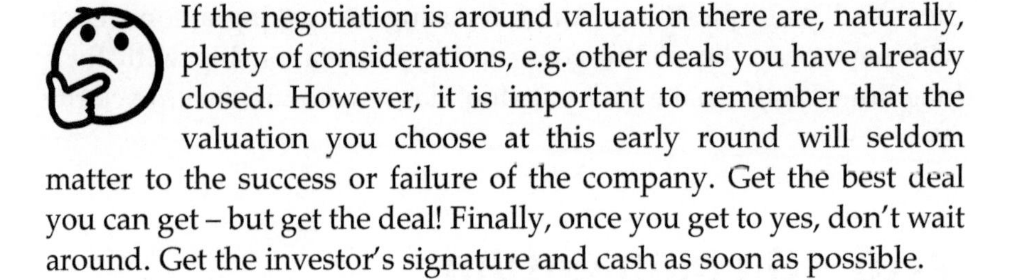

If the negotiation is around valuation there are, naturally, plenty of considerations, e.g. other deals you have already closed. However, it is important to remember that the valuation you choose at this early round will seldom matter to the success or failure of the company. Get the best deal you can get – but get the deal! Finally, once you get to yes, don't wait around. Get the investor's signature and cash as soon as possible.

#118 – Your main focus is...

When I hear why you've started a business and what you'll be doing for the next 12 months or so (with the money you've raised), I hope I'm going to hear that your main focus will be on getting the solution out there, refining it, and solving a problem for more and more customers.

Given the possibility that the business won't survive the next 12 months, I want to hear that (almost) your every waking second is going to be spent getting customer feedback, making improvements and chasing customer revenue. You'll get tempted to spend hours on social media boosting your profile, or commenting on the turbulent life of a founder, or deciding who to be seen with at corporate functions etc., but if you are going to survive then know that you're less important than the product / revenue / customer. That will be taken into account when you seek a next raise.

**Every conversation
you have with a paying customer
is too short.**

#119 – ARR and more about valuation

Investors warm to SaaS companies with strong annual recurring revenue (ARR), and ARR is helpful in agreeing valuation. So, yes, I'm usually all ears to listen to startups that are SaaS and wanting to build ARR. E-commerce businesses can build subscription-based revenue, but it's not quite as meaty. Okay, so start by telling me what problem you're solving with software, and how subscription-based pricing is going to be better for the customer. Tell me why they're going to need it, month in and month out – and why you're going to have to sweat on getting any downtime at all sorted as an emergency.

🤔 Cover off your thoughts / evidence on product / market fit – and then tell me about the numbers (revenue projections and valuation) and assumptions. Kalungi suggests that, throughout 2020, the median SaaS valuation multiple for public companies stood at 16.6x ARR, with private B2B SaaS companies slightly behind at 12.0x ARR. Kalungi shows a rising trend in the value of SaaS businesses.

B2B SaaS companies vary from the traditional business:

- ➡ Most of their revenue is recurring revenue, rather than single purchases.
- ➡ High gross margins as cost-to-service reduces over time.
- ➡ High renewal rates / low churn, which are a key driver of long-term success.
- ➡ Customer service level improvement as they pay.

Yes, you'll have to deliver on these.

(Note: this valuation methodology doesn't come into play until you pass $1m ARR.)

#120 – Loss aversion theory

You might not know what it is – but it means a lot for investors. Kahneman and Teversky showed in 1979 that people tend to prefer to avoid the pain associated with losses rather than seek any pleasure from gains (called 'loss-aversion theory', an element of prospect theory). If you give someone £50 and offer them double or quits on a coin toss, the majority will keep the £50. We'd rather not give up a sure thing to gamble on a potentially great thing. A related part of the theory is that we're less sensitive to losses the more we have. The higher my net worth as an angel, the less concerned I'll be about losing, say, £10,000 compared to someone with a lower net worth (so the theory goes).

Is this theory of any use to you as a founder? Well, I think it is. You might not know the details of my net worth, but it's always useful to ask (either me or other people about me) about what I've invested in. I also find it interesting that founders strongly pitch, and are encouraged to pitch, the upside, i.e. this is a 10x opportunity over five years. That's a great potential return, but loss-aversion theory would indicate that the more confidence you can give an angel (in addition) that it's a relatively safe investment (e.g. size of the market, strength of the team, key advisers involved, LOIs, traction, minimal competition, etc.) the happier they'll be to take a risk.

(Note: Kahneman is one of the most influential economists in the world. Kahneman and Teversky's work is worth further reading.)

#121 – The basics!

As a startup pitching for funding, I'm not sure I want to hear that you're going to beat some unicorn or profitable, revenue-generating multi-national company at their own game. OK, it might sound compelling to the naïve – but, at this point in time, you're barely a minnow's snack. Such vision is admirable, of course, but so future-orientated as to be almost irrelevant at the moment – to you and to me.

Tell me how you are going to achieve the basics – how you'll win business by giving customers value, win a bit more business, be memorable so customers come back to you, stay solvent, get traction, make another raise. You know – the basics!

#122 – So you've got first-mover advantage!

First-mover advantage (FMA) is the competitive advantage a startup gains from being the initial ('first-moving') significant occupant of a market segment. First-mover advantage enables a company or firm to establish technology leadership, strong brand recognition, early customer loyalty and early purchase of resources before other competitors enter the market segment. It has such intuitive appeal that its clear benefit is almost taken for granted. You'll tell me it will give you an insuperable head start. Let me share a note of caution then. Some first-movers clearly don't gain an advantage. Some, for example, become victims of 'free-riding' fast-followers. Second-movers / late movers can study the techniques and strategies of first movers. The late-mover's 'imitation costs' can be much lower than the 'innovation costs' incurred by the first-mover. Successful followers include Airbnb, who built a massive business at the expense of Craigslist, and Amazon overtook books.com in the online bookstore business in the early 1990s.

If you're going to shout 'first-mover advantage' at all your potential investors, then make sure you've investigated the pros and cons and how you'll really control being first to the market, not to the graveyard.

#123 – Founder stories

Founders are always told to 'tell their story', the origin story. I'm going to say something contentious about founder stories. With startups I always find founder stories interesting – sometimes because they are so powerful and sometimes, to be honest, because they're fairly dull.

It's not your fault – perhaps you were sat in the bath and decided that you'd develop a soap bar that didn't go mushy when wet. Well, that's fine. Some founders have truly inspiring stories right at the outset (so, yes, tell it) – but often their story gets better as they grow their company, their struggle to grow the company and beat the odds. The story is about grit and perseverance rather than where their passion or inspiration came from.

Don't worry if you haven't got a 'hero' back-story. Early on, your business is not about you at all. (Okay – I can make a few exceptions!) Or put it another way, your story won't matter much if your product has no market fit. For example, I don't think Airbnb's story would be all that interesting if they'd failed. Tell it if you think it helps – but don't spend too much time on embellishing it. Spend your time on making the best solution you can for customer needs. I might care about your story later – but right now I care more about what you deliver.

#124 – Fake work and momentum

I really love the clarity that the idea of 'fake work' brings to a startup. (Thanks, Sam Altman at YC Combinator). So, let's assume a scenario where you come to me asking for investment and I ask you (a) what you've been doing for the business for the last three months, and (b) what you'll be doing for the next three months.

Altman says you have to prioritise every task you do against how it relates to growing the business. Building, selling and hiring are all growth-oriented. They show clear focus on the key task of growing the business. They keep momentum going, and momentum is everything in a startup. Momentum gets you noticed. Momentum gets you the next raise. Momentum opens the VC door. One of Altman's few startup commandments is 'never let your company lose momentum'. You can search for his full post for the list of work areas he suggests are 'fake work' – not focused on keeping your growth momentum going. You can get distracted by fake work – because it's both easier and more fun that real work. So if I ask about your activity, that's the reason. Investors don't want to invest in a flatlining or meandering business. I want to know if you can grow, keep momentum up and keep yourself accountable.

Momentum is everything in a startup.
Momentum gets you noticed.
Momentum gets you the next raise.
Momentum opens the VC door.
Never let your company lose momentum.
You can't steer a stationary ship.

#125 – It might be as simple as liking*...

Right at the beginning I said that people tend to surround themselves with people like themselves. It's no surprise that we're biased (subconsciously) to invest in people we like and people like us. It's a structural fault in the system. We see this principle being played out often in marketing and advertising. Most adverts will feature individuals designed to appeal to the product's target market. The more the consumer associates with and likes that person, the more likely they are to be influenced by them and purchase the brand. As a fundraising founder you simply need to become liked by those around you and those you are looking to persuade or influence. How you do this is up to you – there are a myriad of ways: paying it forward, engaging in discussion, sharing something of yourself. They key here, though, is that this relationship-building should come first, before asking for money. Cialdini advises that, if you try and become liked once you've started your efforts to influence, then those efforts will fail.

#126 – Be impressive before you raise.

Have you thought of all the things you could do that will cost very little that you can share with angels before you raise? What creative ideas have you thought about? Have you got product design ideas? Are you clear on software functionality? Have you got testers lined up? What team have you put together? What's your initial go-to-market plan looking like? Have you evidenced where your first market(s) will be? Have you got any Letters of Intent (LOI)? Whilst they're non-binding they are still a great sign to an investor that you can validate customer excitement.

All this activity shows very encouraging and persuasive commitment. Angels are always impressed when you can show you've achieved a lot with very little.

---

* Liking is the fifth of Cialdini's 6 Principles of Persuasion.

'If you can't show that you can create $10 out of $1, why will I believe you'll create $10M out of $1M?'

David Frankel
Founder Collective

#127 – Diversity...of thought

Well – we've come full circle really – because I started with the 'system' problem that exists for female founders, black founders and those that haven't had formal higher education. All of that denies diversity of thought and risks leading more homogenous groups to 'groupthink'. What if I asked you how you protected yourself against groupthink? Do you have a groupthink business idea supported by a few like-minded founders that hasn't been objectively tested? Groupthink is easy – it's natural to avoid raising uncomfortable issues. It may cause us to be unpopular. Consensus usually comes after conflict. If your team isn't regularly wrestling with differences of opinion, there's a good chance you've got groupthink going on. If no-one is speaking up, probably someone needs to. Patrick Lencioni calls this 'entering the danger' – a great expression – meaning being willing to challenge the status quo. You can expect angels to probe that – and the openness of your response will be telling.

Startups often emerge from a group of like-minded individuals and I always find it refreshing to see deliberation about diversity emerging early amidst a small team. There is substantial research to show that diversity brings increased profitability and creativity, stronger governance and better problem-solving abilities. It's not yet right up there among top investment criteria, but to me it's really worth pursuing. Tell me about your efforts.

#128 – The 'deal' and the relationship

The transaction between you, the founder, and an angel, the funder, is often referred to as 'the deal'. It can sound a bit impersonal. Sometimes I feel like I've just been through a process to buy a second-hand car – everything is 'friendly' and encouraging until I've passed over the cheque, we shake hands, I get my purchase and then it all goes quiet. That might suit both parties. Some angels are purely passive investors. And, of course, your focus is getting an investment. But calling it 'the deal' can set the wrong tone.

Try looking at it a little differently. Perhaps I hoped I didn't just buy a piece of paper that tells me I own 200 shares in EstrangedAlready Ltd. Perhaps I thought I was buying into a growth story that's only just beginning, and occasionally I need to hear about what happened next. Perhaps I have some ideas I could share or some connections I could make for you? Perhaps an ongoing relationship could be of value to you. I don't mean treat me like a long-lost brother or your soulmate. I just mean let's explore the value of keeping a dialogue going. If you have 10–20 angels on your cap table I guarantee there will be more value there than money.

#129 – So you want to build an ecosystem?

Now that sounds a shiny thing! You can expect me to be excited and nervous for you in equal measure. This is how Greg Sarafin at EY defines an ecosystem:

> 'A business ecosystem is a purposeful business arrangement between two or more entities (the members) to create and share in collective value for a common set of customers. Every business ecosystem has participants, and at least one member acts as the orchestrator of the participants. All members in a business ecosystem, whether orchestrators or participants, have their brands present in the value propositions.'

The principle benefit is that participants can create more value to customers collectively than individually. That's good for you, isn't it? What does 'all members have their brands present' mean? It means when I buy a laptop that's labelled with 'Intel Inside' that the laptop maker and Intel are in an ecosystem and the Intel brand is mentioned alongside the laptop manufacturer.

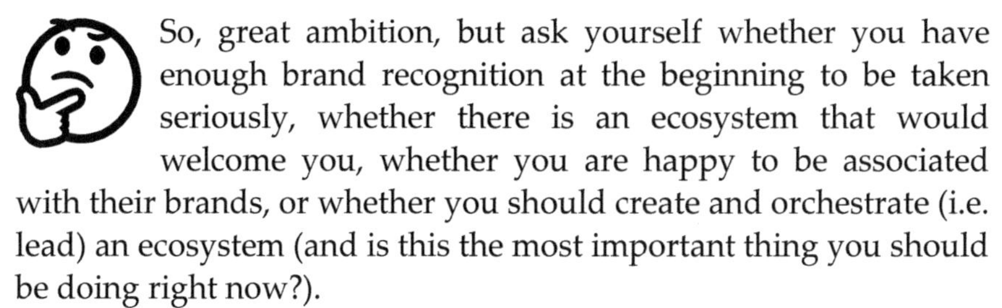

So, great ambition, but ask yourself whether you have enough brand recognition at the beginning to be taken seriously, whether there is an ecosystem that would welcome you, whether you are happy to be associated with their brands, or whether you should create and orchestrate (i.e. lead) an ecosystem (and is this the most important thing you should be doing right now?).

#130 – And have network effects too!

You want to create network effects. One moment while I prick up my ears. Slightly technical definition – it's when the value or utility a user derives from a particular good or service is dependent on the number of users of the same or compatible products. Simply put, more users multiply the value for all users.

Take Facebook / Meta as a well-understood example. As everyone joined it created a bandwagon effect with more people feeling the need to join. People wanted to join the social network that all their friends were on. (Yes – I'm ignoring their more recent problems!). It's a great growth tactic for a startup, but please don't underestimate what it takes to achieve it successfully (on both the demand and supply side). A good network effect involves a positive feedback loop.

The right business model will successfully create network effects if customers take up the work of growing the business for you. Network effect-based businesses fail when they don't reach the critical mass required and so fade away. I'll be very interested to hear (a) whether you fully understand the concept, and (b) how you are planning to make it work sustainably for enough people.

(Note: My first introduction to the concept was the telephone. If you own a telephone, but no one else does, the good is of no value. As more people join the telephone network, the more valuable the telephone becomes to yourself. Your friends also see an increase in value of their telephone because they can now ring you. There is an external benefit of getting this kind of good.)

#131 – Product / market fit

Product / market fit and traction are two terms that both founders and angels struggle with. So if you tell me your product has got them then I'm going to ask you exactly what you have got. Marc Andreessen defines product / market fit as 'being in a good market with a product that can satisfy that market'. A simple analogy for product / market fit is sailing. To take off, you have to build a sail (your product with its value-proposition) and find the wind (market demand) to power it. When there is enough wind (demand) the boat surges forward – you reach an inflection point and the market starts pulling you towards it. Some describe it as a gut feeling as much as anything. Sean Ellis suggests a measure for product / market fit by asking customers this question: 'How disappointed would you be if you could no longer use the [product / service]?' A good fit exists if 40% of surveyed customers indicate that they would be 'very disappointed' if they no longer had access to a particular product or service.*

But just having product / market fit isn't enough. A startup needs to prove it can achieve *venture-scale,* which is more where traction gets mentioned. Traction is really a sales metric – increasing volume and acceleration of sales. So, if you're pre-revenue, you won't have either, but talk it up because these are your aspirations. So I'll be much more enthused if you can not only show me sales growth but an acceleration in sales growth.

132 – How much should you raise?

Guess what – an angel won't know, but many will give an opinion. You're either raising too much or too little! The main thing you have to calculate is where you want to get to with your first raise (call that a milestone or two – because that will largely determine the timing and success of a second raise. For most businesses it's a very optimistic position to take to assume you'll get to profitability or breakeven with one raise. As milestones you'll want a working minimum viable proposition, proof of concept and some traction with revenue. What will it cost to get to that – allowing only a realistically small amount from revenue generated? That can usually be calculated by costs of people (probably your major cost) over a period of time, within or outsourced.

* The Wikipedia entry on product / market fit explains this 40% rule more fully.

The angel's perspective on this is credibility – are you clear on what you want to achieve, does it sound achievable and have you reasonably costed it? You are trading off a number of variables – the milestones you'll achieve, the amount of equity you'll give away (dilution) and what investors will be convinced by. The usual guide is to try to manage getting to your first goal by giving away, at the most, no more than 20% of your company. Better if you can manage in the 10%–15% range. I'll want to see the money take you far enough to justify a next raise.

#133 – On gratitude

You sell me shares in your company. I give you money for them. You say thank you. I say thank you too. End of transaction. It can be like that, it often is – but showing a little gratitude always helps oil the wheels of the relationship. Gratitude produces longer-lasting positivity. Gratitude is not just an action, it is also a positive emotion that serves a biological purpose. It feels more profound when something is given unexpectedly.

Here's a personal example. A little while back, after I'd transferred some money to a founder's nominated bank account for equity, I received a hand-written thank you card in the post, signed by all three co-founders. I was both pleasantly surprised and felt incredibly grateful for my actions being recognised. These small but thoughtful gestures have positive effects for both giver and receiver. This will positively influence my ongoing relations with the founders and the company. It's so simple to do!

> **'Gratitude turns what you have into enough.'**
>
> **Aesop**

#134 – Personal development

What if I asked you what you're reading, and asked your co-founders, and asked anyone you employ? What are you reading, what are you learning from it, how are you growing your horizons? Who are you influenced by? You might say that in whatever time you have spare you binge on Netflix. Surprisingly I find some founders to be against books. They want to learn wholly by doing. That can be expensive learning.

One small piece of advice – look up what Stephen Covey means what he says 'Sharpen the saw'.* How will you help your team sharpen their saws too?

> **'You don't build a business,**
> **you build people.**
> **Then people build the business.'**
>
> **Zig Ziglar**

#135 – 'So, how do I get my money back?' The 'exit strategy' question

You're going to get asked this question a lot – probably every time you pitch. Angels want to get their money returned, that's as you'd expect, but it's also so they can 'play the game' again. What exit really means is 'how will you return money to angels that they invest'.

I wouldn't dignify what most founders think about exit during fundraising with the word 'strategy'. They'd rather not be asked. But you'll have to think about it and give an answer to it. Yes, I know –

---

* From *The Seven Habits of Highly Effective People* by Stephen Covey, 1989.

it's one more thing to think about and you've already got too many things to think about, some of them being too far off into the future. Okay – there are five broad types of exit:

- Acquisition – someone buys you out. Your most likely hope.
- IPO – you get your equity listed on a stock exchange.
- Buy-out – an employee or group, often with some outside help, buys your share of the business from you.
- Merger – you find a 'good fit' partner to merge with to grow a bigger business. For investors it won't release cash but may make you more desirable for acquisition.
- Liquidation – I don't need to spell this out. It's not a plan an angel wants to hear about!

Being able to give some kind of a coherent answer will give investors the confidence that you know what your possible options are several years before any likelihood of the event.

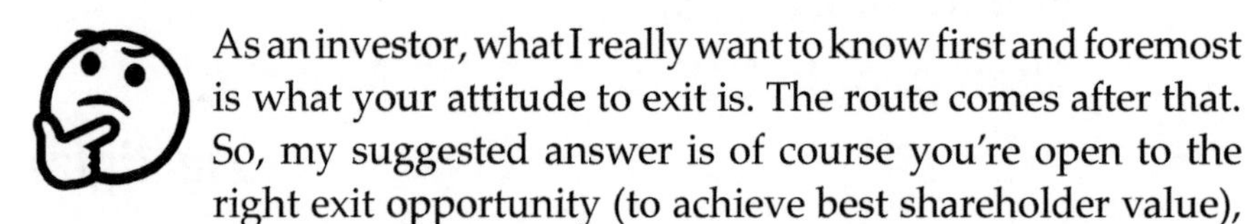

As an investor, what I really want to know first and foremost is what your attitude to exit is. The route comes after that. So, my suggested answer is of course you're open to the right exit opportunity (to achieve best shareholder value), that you know you have to grow successfully to make yourself more attractive, and you'll be pushing your Board to guide you on how to enhance your exit likelihood and opportunities nearer the time. It helps to say that attracting VC interest as you scale will increase the chances of exit happening and you want to get that big. I'd be satisfied with an answer like that.

Let me just slip in one more thought here. If you've done a 'friends and family' round at the beginning of your journey, it's quite possible that those friends and family (some of whom could least afford it but love and trust you) would welcome their money back. Your mum and dad want to retire in some style! Okay, yes, I'm blackmailing you! Being a founder is tough.

I wouldn't dignify what most founders think about exit during fundraising with the word 'strategy'. They'd rather not be asked.

#136 – Angels have visions too

It's important to most angels that we're aligned with what you are trying to do. I mean that in the 'big' and purposeful sense. I might also want to see better things in the world, being done profitably of course.

So, you might have a better chance of finding me and attracting me if you explore my purpose too. I'm not 'doing' what you're doing, of course, but I can certainly take on some 'feelgood' for enabling it to happen. I have my own 'whys'. Why not ask me.

'The most pathetic person in the world is someone who has sight but no vision.'

Helen Keller

#137 – Lead generation

It doesn't matter a whit how big a market you've identified, or how great your product or service is, if you can't capture customers' attention. A quote from Daniel Priestley – 'Attention is the most valuable currency in business – no attention, no business.' Again, this is where you'll need strong marketing input (that I'll obviously ask you about). Priestley goes on the say, 'Everything in business is downstream from lead generation.' It's a statement of the 'bleedin' obvious' that you have to connect customer with solution through marketing. More of the right leads means more sales conversion.

Elsewhere I would have said cashflow is king. Buyers give you cashflow. Leads give you customers. With revenue flowing in you can solve almost any other problem in business. Investors will give you money if you are earning it. Tell me what a lead looks like to you. Tell how you will generate leads. Tell me in detail so that not only I get it, but I know that you get it.

Watson asked Sherlock who shot the victim.

'Somebody with a gun,' Sherlock mocked.

'Well, thank you, Sherlock, for stating the bleeding obvious!' Watson growled.

(Note: this is a made-up quote!)

#138 – On angel groups

General marketing advice says, 'Go where your customers are.' Just as an example, I went to an angel group presentation recently. The screening process was most interesting. If the group has 50 applications to come and pitch, a screening committee shortlists that to about five for actual presentation to the group's angel membership. The criteria used are as you'd expect – clear problem, team information, solution, financial projections, exit plan – and so on. It seems to work well for the benefit of angels – they are presented with a 'curated' and somewhat sanitised list of companies to consider investment in. I'd probably appreciate that as a member. I'd assume that the 'uninvestable' were being filtered out. But also the crazy?

For founders, it's another roadblock to try to negotiate. You have a one in ten chance of your pitch being heard by the people that matter most to you. But what was apparent too, was that there is a 'member's interest filter' too – so if the majority of members don't yet get NFTs or cryptocurrency proposals you won't get heard either. Or if it's just a very exciting proposal but you haven't ticked another box well enough, you won't get heard. So, don't rely on this being your only route to investors. Going where angels are means going everywhere they are.

#139 – Let's climb the value ladder

Founders – show me your value ladder, please. Yes, okay, you might not have one on day one, but you'd do well to develop one. What is such a thing? It's a two-dimensional method of visually mapping out your product / service offering in ascending order of value and price – a 'value staircase' if you like. Being able to offer value at different price brackets means you don't leave money on the table.

Think of a phone package or TV package, or going into a carpet shop. There's something for everyone's budget. If you're going to get to a multi-million-pound turnover then just 'one-product, one-price' probably isn't going to cut it for you. And tell me that you'll always put value first before price.

An example of a value ladder:

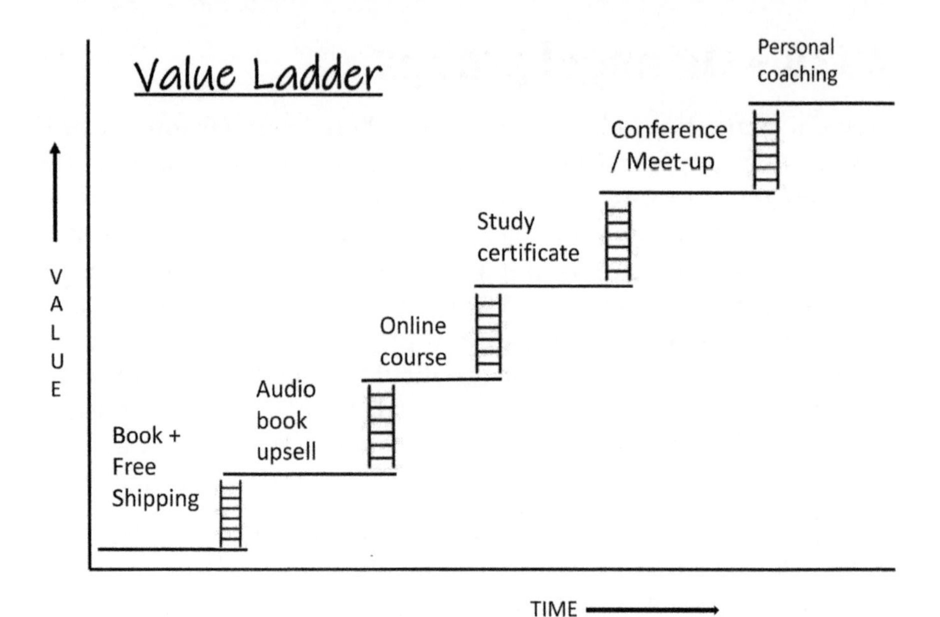

#140 – Be astute – plan for the next raise too

Many founders say the second raise is harder than the first, and they wonder why. The second raise tests something other than, no, more than, the first raise. First raises can be a bit 'soft' on founders – they focus on the problem, your vision, your team, a vague go-to-market strategy and financial projections.

Next-round funders, and that may be a VC, will want to know how far you got with the first-raise money, how you de-risked your initial market assumptions, and what 'excuses' you'll come up with. Next-round funders have one main concern – however you describe it – that you've got traction or momentum and it's shown by growing revenue. That requires disciplined focus.

Tell me how you are going to make sure your seed raise is not going to get sucked into the wrong places and it's going to deliver momentum. Your seed round ideas may soon become irrelevant – because you need to answer to investors how you will sell to customers. Prove to investors that your (prospective) customers have an appetite for your product above all else. That's what shrewd investors will want to see. Me too (I think I'm shrewd!).

Hope isn't a strategy.

#141 – The perfect and the 'good-enough'

Do you have a fear of failure? It would be entirely natural. How strong is it? It's not uncommon to find that talking to customers makes a founder's fear of failure worse, in case they say your product isn't quite the thing you hope it is. That can drive you to spend more time on trying to perfect the product because of that fear. See where I'm going with all this? Perfectionism has two sides – an excellence-seeking side which pushes you to constantly improve a product, and a failure-avoiding side which might stop you from learning from talking with customers. Sometimes we don't just build an MVP and sometimes we hope that our effort put into the product will somehow blow customers away (so we don't have to talk to them). Is your MVP much more than an MVP? Have you not been able to control the time put into product development? That's what devs tend to do; use up your time. Have you got 'feature creep' for example? That's where your money goes.

So, please tell me you've got control of this with the funding you'll raise. How are you actually going to control this? I'll be interested.

(Note: You might enjoy reading more about the Minimum Lovable Product (MLP), which takes customers adoring a product as the minimum starting point (not merely tolerating it), but still emphasises 'minimum'.)

Don't let the perfect be the enemy of the good.

#142 – What exactly is your fundraising strategy?

Excuse me for asking – because I'm guessing that if you want to raise, say, £250k you've got some sort of plan (because I'm not going to be filling your round on my own).

So tell me about it. At least give me an overview. Where are you looking for investors? Have you got a lead investor, or a few people in mind? Have you split the sum down into different segments – strategic investors, other angels, possibly grants, any Micro VC input, possibility of debt or loans? Have you set any minimum investment levels, e.g. for angels you expect at least a £20k contribution?

Have you got a content plan for what you're going to aim at all these people? LinkedIn, Twitter, YouTube, email marketing, newsletters, etc. Have you all the documents you'll need – pitchdeck, cap table, financial forecasts, shareholders agreement, business plan, more detailed team profiles, etc.

Tell me who is taking charge of fundraising and what main things they will be doing. Do they have a daily target / weekly target? Just curious (about your chances of success)!

How will you keep momentum going? Don't leave things too late.

#143 – Butter me up!

We all have our own sense of self-worth. We enjoy being recognised for something and being flattered for that. I don't mean you should tell me 'You look nice.' Don't get banal. But if you tell me you enjoyed reading something I've written or you'd value my opinion on something I have expertise in, it makes me feel positive (and it doesn't feel like deliberate ego-stroking). When you've found the investors you'd really like, then let them know you'd be very interested to have them alongside you. Research them, find a great reason why you want them and share it with them, such as you think you might both have shared values about X, or you'd heard they were really helpful to Y, or you'd value their expertise on Z.

There's nothing wrong with making us angels feel good!

#144 – Dealing with 'no'

Investors have a lot of different ways to say no. We say things like 'not enough traction' or 'not sure of the product / market fit' or 'not a big enough market'. One thing is for sure, it might just be a gut feeling that we can't put a finger on. The hardest thing for a founder can be getting to grips with being turned down, possibly not liking or agreeing with the reason, sometimes not even knowing, and being okay with it. You've put so much into getting to that point, but you've got to pick yourself up and press on.

Paul Graham, Y Combinator, likes to say, 'If the soda is empty, stop making that awful sucking sound with the straw.' But remember, 'no' is no from one person only. 'No' isn't necessarily permanent either. The investor might be a 'yes' another time, so part on the best possible terms and try and leave the door open. You've no need to tell other investors you've had refusals.

#145 – The best (and worst) ways to meet investors

In an article in Incafrica.com in 2014, Jeff Yasuda, a former VC, listed six ways to get to investors – from worst to best. Here's a summary:

6. Cold call / Cold email
He never responded to entrepreneurs who cold called or cold emailed him. He was inundated with requests. Brilliant assumption here: 'If an entrepreneur failed to exhibit basic resourcefulness to get at least a lukewarm intro, my assumption was that the entrepreneur was probably not resourceful enough to get to a potential customer or business partner.' Avoid cold calls and emails at all costs.

5. Intro from an investor who has passed
Imagine receiving intros from fellow investors who say, 'We're not interested in this company, but maybe you are ...?' Not good enough for me but good enough for you? Generally avoid.

4. Intro from an existing investor or adviser of the company
These are generally pretty good introductions from someone who knows the company well. The one downside is that the introducer knows MORE about the company. The introduction does not come from a truly unbiased and disinterested party. That may give a new investor pause.

3. Intro from a trusted entrepreneur who has been funded
An entrepreneur who has been funded probably has several connections with other funding sources with whom they spoke when they went through their financing. Worth cultivating those relationships. It's worth looking at the companies VCs have funded and cultivating a relationship with their founders.

2. Intro from a trusted entrepreneur who has exited
Investors sit up and take note when successful (exited) entrepreneurs make recommendations to them. Investors often think that proven entrepreneurs have an even better sense as to what it takes to be successful.

And the best intro:

1. When a VC chases you because he / she is hearing about how well you are doing from customers, partners, and the press
Reverse inquiry is the best. You can try waiting – but you have to build up a lot of buzz and momentum.

There's a very interesting lesson here – go and seek introductions to investors from trusted and successful entrepreneurs. Over to you!

'If an entrepreneur failed to exhibit basic resourcefulness to get at least a lukewarm intro, my assumption was that the entrepreneur was probably not resourceful enough to get to a potential customer or business partner.'

Jeff Yasuda, former VC

#146 – On price-making

Rarely can a startup be a price-maker from the outset. You can't defy a basic rule of economics (see Marshall's model of 'perfect competition'). A price-maker is someone who has enough market power to change the market price of goods or services. A company with market power has a near-monopolistic control in the market – it can raise prices without losing its customers to competitors. Think Microsoft, Games Workshop or Diageo. A 'no brand' startup, even with a great product, will face high levels of scepticism and substitution.

Best to accept that you'll be a price-taker (accept prevailing market prices) until you can justify otherwise and build that into your projections. If you can get to profitability at that level, then you'll be more investable.

#147 – Where's the social proof?

Most people are happier to be followers than leaders – but they need to see the norms a social group is conforming to. Herein lies the power of social proof* (whether that be star ratings, testimonials, net promoter scores, whatever). Experiments with recycling show that we recycle more if we believe our neighbours are recycling. A classic example of social proof is that hotel signage that says '8 out of 10 hotel guests choose to reuse their towels' is far more effective at influencing and persuading than signs that simply say 'reusing your towel helps to save the environment' (This is nudge theory in practice).

What examples can you show of social proof that will influence investors? It may not be purchaser satisfaction or buyer scores at the early stage, it might be user sign-ups to an app in development or retailers to a platform. It could be the views of unbiased experts. Think imaginatively about the social proof metrics you can conjure up to bring along the doubters.

---

* The last of Cialdini's 6 Principles of Persuasion is consensus, or social proof.

#148 – On overconfidence

I love to hear founders sounding confident about their product or service and that the market is strong. Let me ask you some questions. They may be difficult. First, how many real customers have you talked to in the last three months? That should be easy – it's just a number. Next, how have you become convinced that those customers really want your product? What have you shown them? Have they ordered it? Paid for it? Given you a letter of intent or other assurances?

In your efforts to raise money you've probably talked a lot about your market to investors, but maybe not customers. Try and evidence the real strength of your market and justify your confidence.

#149 – You tell me you're jumping into the (blue) ocean?

You might excite me if you can convince me you know what you are talking about.

W Chan Kim and Renée Mauborgne, professors at INSEAD, published Blue Ocean Strategy in 2004. They claim to describe a different approach to growth. They argue 'cutthroat competition results in nothing but a bloody red ocean of rivals fighting over a shrinking profit pool'. Companies should instead look for new market spaces – the blue ocean – and ways to reinvent an industry. In short, they should avoid head-to-head competition, focus on innovation, and give customers something unique and of immense value. Blue oceans are uncontested, growing market opportunities; red oceans are overdeveloped, saturated markets. They argue that companies in a blue ocean market will have more success, face fewer risks and secure greater profits.

That's beguilingly simple – so tell me how your idea does that.

Cirque du Soleil is the most commonly cited example of a famous blue ocean success. In the early 1980s a bunch of 'crazy Canadians' started asking what a modern circus could look like. The traditional circus 'spectacle' was based on clowns and performing animals, the target audience was children and families, and fun and laughter were the objective. Cirque du Soleil did away with live animal acts, enabling the company to reduce its cost base. It introduced live music and a storyline, inspired by the world of theatre. It changed the 'spectacle' to extraordinary and astonishing human physical skills. It shifted the customer base to primarily adults and corporate clients willing to pay higher ticket prices than parents. It created a more sophisticated experience and reinvented the circus for a new market, with low cost and differentiation and without competition. It has since gone on to entertain more than 155 million people in over 300 cities.

Other examples of successful Blue Ocean Strategy companies include Nintendo Wii, iTunes, Backroads and Yellow Tail.

If you have a genuine example of a blue ocean business then SHOUT about it!

Red Ocean Strategy	Blue Ocean Strategy
Exploit **existing** demand	Create and capture **new** demand
Compete in **existing** market space	Create **uncontested** market space
Beat the competition	Make the competition **irrelevant**
Make the value-cost trade-off	**Break** the value-cost trade-off
Align every company activity with its strategic choice of **differentiation** or of **low cost**	Align every company activity with its strategic choice of **differentiation and low cost**

(Note: The value-cost trade-off is the conventional belief that companies can either create greater value to customers at a higher cost or create reasonable value at a lower cost. The strategy choice is seen as making a choice between differentiation and low cost. Breaking that trade-off means delivering high value at reasonable cost.)

In short, a blue ocean company should avoid head-to-head competition, focus on innovation and give customers something unique and of immense value.

#150 – I can't leave without mentioning dopamine...

Dopamine is the pleasure molecule released in our brain when we do pleasurable things – like eat, have sex, drink alcohol. When released, we experience a strong sensation of pleasure and, of course, we will want to repeat that experience. Consider this – we go to a meeting. Tea and coffee are served. But this time someone has gone overboard on the biscuit budget. There are individually foil-wrapped chocolate wafer biscuits on plates on the table (you know the brand you like!). The anticipation is more than enough for dopamine to kick in. Large amounts are released when two things happen:

- We think about the pleasurable experience.
- There is a realistic opportunity that we will be able to have the pleasurable experience (there is true anticipation).

We start to experience pleasure before we've even unwrapped the biscuit.

So think about how you can give angels a strong feeling of anticipation. If you just send me a pitchdeck out of the blue, that's short-circuited all the anticipation, hasn't it? If you warm me up by sharing with me what you are working on, then tell me you think you're there, you can build anticipation. You might give me more excitement that way. I might enjoy the engagement with you more that way. Or at the start of a live pitch try 'foreshadowing' (what authors do to indicate something exciting is going to happen). Try saying something like, 'Shortly I'm going to reveal to you an amazing investment opportunity – but first I need to tell you about this problem.'

Why not you use my own brain to get to me as well as yours?

Conclusion

Founders – we're at the end. I don't know what you thought you were going to get when you picked this book up. What I wanted to give you was a great many insights about business angels, insights that most founders don't have. In business we call that competitive advantage. I hope you can make the best use it.

Often founders are led to believe a simple manta – that the proposition is about 'the founder, the idea and the market'. I'm not going to argue with that – always nice to have a simple rubric, except that it's just too simple. I hope I've shown you that.

> **'One reason people succeed is that they have knowledge that other people don't.'**
>
> **Tony Robbins**

I'll attempt to summarise here what I see as the really important lessons in the book.

The fundraising 'system' you find yourself in has many flaws and biases. It is up to you, founder, whether you follow its many rules and conventions – but most of them are not there for your benefit anyway so don't feel you have to abide by them.

The biggest flaw is the widespread belief that you start your fundraising journey with a pitchdeck. No relationship-building needed. This is so wrong-headed. If you take nothing else away from this book, I'll be happy.

Another assumption founders suffer from is that you have to apply for funding through an angel group or only from people who declare themselves as angels. There are many, many ways to get to know and get in front of angels (and, of course, the premise of this book – to influence them differently), or to engage people who could be first-time investors. Einstein's definition of madness comes to mind – keeping doing what you've always done and expecting a different outcome.

Another convention I would challenge is not speaking to VCs at the outset – because there's perhaps 1 in 100 chance that they would be interested even if you have minimal revenue. They might give you useful leads even if they don't invest. That's more a matter of the time you've got and prioritising it. The ROI is low, but who knows what interest or valuable future relationships you might form. Another insight is asking angels for help or advice rather than money. It's a bit of an ego thing. We love to be asked to help, to give advice, etc. and when we see the potential in what you've got, that can lead us to investing. Am I making the importance of relationships clearer?

Next, marketing is moving away from mass-marketing (what I've called shotgun marketing earlier) to much more targeted marketing. People-based marketing talks about personalising your approach and trying to meet people where they are. Conventionally you'd find angels at angel groups, on online angel networks, listing sites and self-identifying on social networks like LinkedIn. They won't all be there, and they won't especially welcome approaches from strangers. So consider what else you can do. Here's some ideas to begin with:

- Angels usually know other angels. Ask for introductions from the ones you do know. Ask successful entrepreneurs who funded them. Ask for intros to funders. Funders particularly welcome those.
- Make people aware of what you are doing before you need money, so that you build a relationship and a following. Almost every approach I get from a founder I get via LinkedIn from someone who has never been in touch with me until he or she needs money. It's the wrong time to start building a relationship. Use LinkedIn

to share what you're interested in building and what your values are (in general terms) and see who comes forward. Build your network early.

- Develop relationships with people who might know high net worth individuals – such as accountants, solicitors, company owners.
- Find company owners who have just sold businesses who might be sitting on a large pile of money. Entrepreneurs often become angels in these circumstances.
- Join local networking groups. Ask people about what they do and let reciprocity work – they'll ask you about what you do. There's your chance.

Remember what I said earlier about creating a great first impression. One thing we all do after we've met someone online or in person is check their LinkedIn profile. Make sure that's impressive, and up to date, too. Your 'about' section and your posts are a place to convince people (or turn them off).

The vast field of psychology provides many insights. Take loss-aversion theory. Angels are gamblers, no doubt about it, but if you can just add a little sense of a 'safety net' feel to the proposition then that helps. Being able to claim tax relief on EIS and SEIS-qualifying deals sweetens the pill a little. Nudging investors to invest (I've had 15 of your astute colleagues saying yes to this) is both using 'groupthink' and 'nudge theory'. Some angels will relish the opportunity of being the first investor across the line – a little 'individualist' streak. You can potentially use groupthink to your advantage – get your pitch in front of a group of angels and those that really like it may carry some of the waverers towards you.

I've mentioned other cognitive biases you might use to give you an edge:

- Confirmation bias (interpreting what we see as what we want to see). For example, angels very much want to see a proposition that looks like a success story, so do that – make it look like a success story.

- ➡ Representativeness bias (seeing a charismatic or persuasive founder as representative of the most successful entrepreneurs we can think of). Just be as engaging and persuasive as you can and let their minds do the work for you.
- ➡ Survivorship bias (the tendency we have of focusing on successful people, businesses or strategies, and (subconsciously) ignoring those that failed). Present yourself as supremely confident and win their attention.
- ➡ Halo effect (the tendency to become blinded by the good in something or somebody and not seeing any of its / their faults). This could, for example, be playing to 'shiny object syndrome' – the tendency some people have to continually chase new trends, new opportunities and new ideas without evaluating their benefit first.

Remember – you are not responsible for the interpretations or thought patterns others have.

I'd strongly suggest you take Cialdini's principles to heart – work on getting to be liked, work on reciprocity and 'paying it forward'. Build your authority and credibility. Build your social proof. All are shown to work.

Next, play to our sense of risk-taking. We are all risk-takers. We want to hear you say you'll 'go big' and go 'all-in'. We want to hear that big panoramic vision, to know what you are fighting for. Put the excitement into your story. Find the emotional hooks and hot-buttons that will turn us on, e.g. there's a thrill-ride to be had here. Go back and read about dopamine, particularly in anticipation of excitement. Some of us enjoy the status dimension of being called an angel too, particularly if it leads on to other roles like Non-Executive Director or Chairman. Offering roles (to the right people) alongside a decent ticket-size investment can really help some angels make a decision.
Find out what you can about our motivations for investing. It's rarely just about money. We're all different and have different drivers. Remember WIIFM (What's In It For Me). Make an effort to get to know us individually and explore how your proposition fits with our needs. It probably will be about money but not only that.

Be honest. Please don't make stuff up. I've given examples already. Is your proposition really disruptive? Have you really tested a particular market? Are you sure about the need? How? Has your team got the skills it claims? Go back and look at the jugular questions I asked.

Remember the importance of keeping momentum up. We will be swayed by evidence of your momentum and energy.

I've mentioned ego-stroking too. Use ways to make me feel good about working with you. Don't overdo it. Don't make it obvious – keep it subtle – but I warm to a bit of buttering up.

Lastly – I must have mentioned storytelling many times in this book. I'm obviously a fan! You must learn how to tell a story well. I really mean it. In fiction-writing, stories usually begin with a problem or dilemma, they have plots and characters, they follow a story arc. They end with a resolution. The real power of good storytelling is that it engages our emotions. It creates an empathy with the protagonist (you) that draws us into the story and makes us want to go with you.

You must learn how to tell a story well.

So, tell me the problem clearly. Make it make me sit up in my seat. It's the 'story of now' – what is the urgent challenge that you are trying to inspire me to take action on with you, and how can we begin **NOW**! The resolution compares to your vision and mission – what will make something so much better for your target audience (remember the persona people?) if you can just give them X product or service, and what they'll get back too. Your team are the characters in your story. Have the best cast you can. The plot is how you unfold the events – the series of actions you'll take in the order you'll take them, i.e. the execution of your strategy. Sprinkle your story with smaller stories – the individuals you've helped and their testimonials, the struggles you've found customers face, the star-ratings you've earned so far. Work out what 'hot buttons' you are trying to press. Tell your investors what part they could play in the story. Tell them what their investment will achieve – how it will help what you are fighting for. Your story is how you weave it all together – you, the idea (problem and solution) and the market, into one compelling narrative.

Of course, do the pitch-polishing – that goes without saying. Make it the best communication tool you can. That's not really the difficult bit. You can have a great pitchdeck and still not get anywhere. What you really need to do is get in my head, start to think like me, second-guess me, take over my thinking, use your brain to make my brain (the cognitive, the emotional, the chemical, etc.) work for you not against you. Remember angel empathy? I hope I've given you plenty of insights to do all that and it will yield the funding you need. I hope I've given you the edge.

I wish you good fortune.

About the Author

Phil McSweeney is a business angel, alongside a portfolio of other related interests. He's a company Chair, a Non-Executive Director of several companies, an adviser to founders and Boards (primarily on growth strategy), a mentor, a trained executive coach, an educator, a course developer and a published author. He's met hundreds of founders and worked with and invested in a few dozen of them across a variety of sectors. He's helped several companies plan and implement their fundraising strategies. He's also met hundreds of angels and has been an active member of several angel groups.

He's put this book together from an angel's perspective to help founders better understand the dynamic between them and angels, from idea conception through to exit. It's based on his own experience and research, including interviews with many angel colleagues. He wants to help more founders use insights into how angels think to radically improve their chances of raising funds. He enjoys writing, blogging, contributing on LinkedIn and helping people through his writing.

He's been an investor through most of his adult life and became an angel investor after redundancy in his early 50s. He very much enjoyed getting into the whole startup experience after 30 years in the NHS, first as a clinician and finally as a Director of a Trust.

Outside of all the startup activity he's married with two grown-up daughters and a granddaughter. In his spare time, he enjoys the company of family and friends, talking about retirement, gardening and, of course, writing.

Index